A STRANGE CAMPAIGN

THE BATTLE FOR MADAGASCAR

RUSSELL PHILLIPS

Foreword by
PETER CADDICK-ADAMS

SHILKA PUBLISHING

CONTENTS

FOREWORD

PETER CADDICK-ADAMS

I have studied the Normandy invasion for much of my life as a professional military historian. They're sadly no longer with us now, but I've been fortunate to encounter and interview hundreds who fought there and discuss with them — and numerous academic and military colleagues — the reasons for the success of those far-off days of June 1944. We've put our feet up at the numerous hostelries that line the French coast, and over *moules-frites* and the odd (sometimes very odd) glass of wine pondered all the moving parts that made Operation Overlord, and Neptune, its maritime counterpart, so successful.

My mind is always attuned to the fact that the achievement of Eisenhower, Montgomery and Ramsay in providing the springboard into Europe that led to the downfall of Nazi Germany was due to the disaster of Operation Jubilee. The Dieppe landing of 19th August 1942 saw a multi-national, tri-service force receive a huge setback, losing thirty-three landing craft, a destroyer that had to be scuttled, twenty-nine tanks, 106 aircraft and 4,384 killed, wounded or taken captive. There is much debate about the lessons learned from Dieppe, and how they influenced Overlord. Mountbatten — head of Combined Operations at the time — would claim that the latter would have been impossible without the former. Others have observed merely that Jubilee, if nothing else, 'taught us how *NOT* to do a major assault from the sea'.

Sitting 250 miles off the African coast in the Indian Ocean, the world's second-largest island has always been on the fringes of my consciousness as somewhere else that also received an amphibious assault during the Second World War. To my shame, probably because I have yet to set foot there, I paid little attention to Madagascar — a Vichy French colony at the time, and therefore hostile to Britain — until I read Russell Phillips' excellent volume describing its very necessary occupation in 1942.

In *A Strange Campaign* we discover why Madagascar's location was so important strategically. That it was vital the Allies owned its deep water ports, controlling access both to India and the Suez Canal. In Vichy French hands, the fear was that its Governor and garrison might fall under German or (more likely) Japanese domination. Hence, the first large-scale combined operation of the Second World War by an Allied sea, land, and air force. From the point of view of timing, Operation Ironclad, the initial capture of its major port, Diego-Suarez (now Antsiranana), was significant, beginning only fourteen weeks before Dieppe, on 5th May 1942, yet with a very different outcome.

When compared to Overlord, the planning for Ironclad seems almost amateurish, but it was still felt to be sufficiently important to merit the deployment of a battleship, two carriers with nearly one hundred embarked aircraft, and forty-three cruisers, destroyers, and other warships, at a time when British naval resources were hugely stretched in the Mediterranean, North Atlantic and Pacific. Interestingly, *A Strange Campaign* relates that it was at Madagascar the *Bachaquero*, Britain's first LST (a merchantman converted into tank landing ship), deposited a dozen tanks on a hostile shore. That a flung-together infantry division of three brigades, plus No. 5 Commando, was deployed in ten assault and troopships, splashing ashore from LCAs (assault landing craft) also underlines the point about scale. This was no mere commando raid on a small island but a major combined operation, when Britain was still exploring the nature of amphibious warfare.

Despite the remarkably light casualty bill of 500 killed or wounded (slightly more dying from disease than combat), *A Strange Campaign* tells how this became a major British success in a year peppered with military reverses. The only reason the whole of Madagascar was not captured until November 1942 was it was not attempted. Initially, it was thought the Vichy forces would surrender, but they proved to be more resilient — ironically holding out for longer than did their native France in 1940 — and had to be isolated and reduced piecemeal, but at minimal cost.

Did lessons flow from the initial success at Madagascar to the planning for Dieppe? Almost certainly not; the time frame was too brief and the nature of the assault, using troops eventually bound for India, was ad hoc. The Dieppe raid was originally planned for early July as Operation Rutter, cancelled then reinstated as Jubilee. However, I ask myself, did Ironclad in any way pave the way for Overlord? The answer is that I am sure that it did.

Some of the initial landings at Madagascar were

hampered by assault shipping being unable to deliver troops and vehicles onto their chosen beaches. The establishment of Combined Operations Pilotage Parties (COPPs) in September 1942 would solve this. Their special forces canoeists conducted secret reconnaissance of potential landing beaches for all the major assaults, beginning with other Vichy French outposts in North Africa on 8th November 1942 (Operation Torch), and such mishaps were never repeated.

That's not all. Apart from the presence of the first LST — America would go on to mass produce over 1,000, without which the Normandy landings would have been impossible — we see at Madagascar the extensive work of SOE (Special Operations Executive) personnel operating behind the lines. Their intelligence was not always trusted, but by the time of Overlord the Allies had learned to trust their spies. *A Strange Campaign* narrates the use of commandos in conjunction with infantry landings, and the first Allied use of dummy paratroops. The flotilla of assault ships, carrying smaller landing craft, included the Royal Ulsterman, which would go on to take part in Torch, Husky and Avalanche (1943) and Overlord. Her companion, the Winchester Castle, also landed troops in Torch and Avalanche, and then in Southern France for Operation Dragoon on 15 August 1944. Thus, in the successful Operation Ironclad of 1942, we have the seeds of success of all the other major amphibious landings in Europe during the war.

This is why I commend Russell Phillips' *A Strange Campaign* to you. Ignore Madagascar at your peril. I leaned much from this volume and I hope you will too. As a result, my first act will be to visit the island when I can and combine some military history with tropical sun.

Although an obscure-seeming footnote to Second World War military history, Madagascar is actually a key event in the evolutionary process that culminated with victory in Normandy two years later.

Professor Peter Caddick-Adams, March 2021

ACKNOWLEDGMENTS

My grateful thanks to Colonel Dudley Wall MSM, MMM, SADF, and Chris Sams for their help with research. Thanks are also due to Paul Mayer for clarifications and corrections regarding his parents, Percy Mayer OBE and Berthe Mayer MBE. Finally, my thanks to Dewi Hargreaves for the maps and Bruno Bord for help with French spelling and terminology. Any mistakes are all mine.

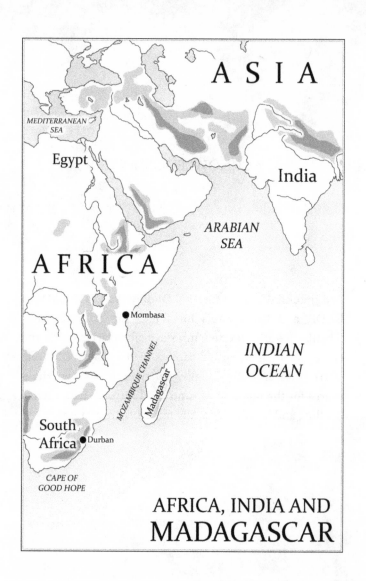

ASIA

MEDITERRANEAN
SEA

Egypt

India

ARABIAN
SEA

AFRICA

Mombasa

INDIAN
OCEAN

MOZAMBIQUE CHANNEL

Madagascar

South
Africa ● Durban

CAPE OF
GOOD HOPE

AFRICA, INDIA AND
MADAGASCAR

INTRODUCTION

On 5th May 1942, British troops landed on the island of Madagascar. The opposing forces weren't German, Italian, or Japanese — they were French. Most people think of Britain and France as allies during the Second World War, but the relationship between the two countries was much more complex. To explain why Britain invaded Madagascar, we need to go back to 1940.

When France fell in 1940, Marshal Pétain formed a new French government, based at the spa town of Vichy. This new government signed an armistice with Germany, leaving them theoretically neutral in the wider war. But in practice the Germans made ever-greater demands of Vichy France, and with three-fifths of France under German occupation, the French could not realistically refuse. By 1942, not only were Britain and France no longer allies, relations between the two countries were very strained.

Defeat in the Battle of France engendered a lot of bad feeling between the two nations. The French complained that the British had favoured their own troops over the French in the evacuation at Dunkirk in May and June 1940. This was true initially, when the French had not decided to evacuate. Once the French agreed to take part, the British took roughly equal numbers of British and French troops. The numbers of men taken off the beaches — 140,000 French and 198,000 British — reflect this.

After Dunkirk, as the Germans began attacking south, the French demanded support from the Royal Air Force. They wanted ten fighter squadrons sent to France immediately, with another ten to follow later. The British, wanting to ensure that they had sufficient aircraft to defend Britain, declined. Still hoping to keep France in the fight, Britain sent the 52nd Division to France on 6th June 1940, and planned to send the Canadian Division on the 11th, with a third division to follow later.

At a meeting on 11th June, both British and French politicians and generals accepted that they had lost the Battle of France. Churchill was keen for the French to continue the fight, suggesting that street fighting in Paris could bleed the German army dry. Every Frenchman present opposed the idea, and they declared Paris an open city the next day, to save it from the damage that would ensue from such a battle.

Weygand, the French commander-in-chief, demanded that the British send all their fighter aircraft to France immediately, believing it was France's only hope. Churchill refused, saying that the British would need them when the Luftwaffe attacked Britain. He countered with a suggestion that the French could base themselves in North Africa, where they had a significant army, and continue the fight from their empire.

One of Churchill's primary concerns was the powerful

French fleet. If it was allowed to fall under German control, it could cause significant difficulties for the Royal Navy. Admiral Darlan, Chief of Staff of the French Navy, assured him that France would not allow her fleet to fall into German hands.

Over the next few days, the French government started to seriously consider asking for an armistice. The idea of moving the government to North Africa and continuing the fight from there was also considered. The British, realising that keeping troops in France simply put them at risk for no gain, evacuated their troops and remaining aircraft between 15th and 18th June 1940. This gave further ammunition to those that blamed Britain for France's defeat. Some suggested that Britain essentially considered France to be defeated, and that the alliance was therefore over.

Earlier, in March, the French had wanted Britain to sign a declaration that neither country would seek a separate armistice or peace treaty. Britain had agreed to this with no objections, and now France found themselves in the embarrassing position of asking Britain to allow them to renege on this declaration. Britain agreed, but with the significant condition that the French fleet be "sailed forthwith to British harbours pending negotiations". Britain later requested that the French air force should fly its aircraft to North Africa to put them out of German reach, and that allied troops (Czechs, Poles, Belgians) still in France should be sent to Britain. To French eyes, this all looked suspiciously like Britain trying to loot the French corpse for military hardware and troops.

In a last desperate attempt to keep France in the war, Britain sent a message suggesting that the two countries should unite. The idea was rejected as yet another attempt by Britain to acquire French arms. Far from keeping

France in the war, the message led to the collapse of the Reynaud government. Marshal Pétain formed a new government, and immediately sought an armistice, which was signed in the Compiègne Forest in France on 22nd June 1940.

In the twenty-first century, Madagascar is valued for its unique wildlife. In 1940, little heed was paid to its ecology or heritage, but the Nazis saw other potential value in the island. At this time, the Nazi solution to the so-called "Jewish question" was deportation rather than wholesale slaughter. Madagascar had been discussed as a potential destination for Europe's Jews as early as 1938. So German occupation of Madagascar was a distinct possibility, not for military reasons, but so that they could forcibly evict millions of Jews from Europe to the island.

One of the terms of the armistice was that French warships not earmarked for colonial duties were to be recalled to France. Some of these ships were in ports under British control, having sought sanctuary while France was still fighting. Two battleships, four cruisers, several submarines, and around 200 smaller vessels were in Britain. One battleship, four cruisers, and various support ships were in the port of Alexandria in Egypt, which was under British control.

Admiral Darlan, the new Minister of Marine, wanted the ships in British ports to return to France, and sooner rather than later. He had no intention of them serving alongside German ships, but he didn't want them being used by the British either. The British, for their part, still feared that they would reinforce the German navy, with or without Darlan's cooperation, so they refused to let them leave. The issue came to a head with Operation Catapult, which was planned to deal with the various parts of the French fleet simultaneously.

British sailors and Royal Marines boarded every French ship in a British port at 04:30 on 3rd July 1940. The hope was to avoid bloodshed, so although some boarders were armed with pistols or rifles, others had pickaxe handles. They boarded in overwhelming numbers in an attempt to intimidate the French sailors into compliance. In most cases, they avoided bloodshed as intended, but the large submarine *Surcouf* battened down the hatches before the British could board. The British managed to open the conning tower hatch from outside and board the submarine, but the French officers refused to leave. There was a tense stand-off until a French officer opened fire with his pistol. After a brief firefight, the French accepted the inevitable and surrendered. Two British officers and one seaman had been killed, and a second seaman was wounded. A French warrant officer had been killed, and one officer wounded.

In Alexandria, the French and British vice-admirals, Godfroy and Cunningham, had a good personal relationship, and came to an agreement: Godfroy would not try to sail without informing Cunningham. In return, Cunningham would not try to take control of the French ships. Neither of their superiors were happy with the arrangement. Eventually, Cunningham persuaded Godfroy to mothball his ships with reduced crews, the rest being repatriated to France or allowed to join de Gaulle's Free French, the military forces of the French government-in-exile.

The French were not happy about their ships in British ports being boarded and taken over, and their ships in Alexandria being blockaded. These actions paled into insignificance, however, compared to what happened at Mers El Kébir.

The French navy had a large and powerful force docked at Mers El Kébir in Algeria. As part of Operation Catapult, Admiral Sir James Somerville sailed with Force H to Mers El Kébir. His orders were to deliver an ultimatum that would require the French ships to be sailed to Britain or the West Indies, or to be sunk. If the French refused to do any of these things, he was to destroy them. Somerville started negotiations, having decided on a deadline of 15:00. Gensoul, the French admiral, refused to speak to Somerville's representative Captain Holland directly, and sent a lieutenant instead.

Gensoul refused to bow to any of the British demands, and said that the French ships would defend themselves if fired upon. Twenty minutes before the deadline, however, he sent a signal saying that he would personally meet Somerville's representative. Somerville suspected correctly that Gensoul was playing for time, but in the hope of avoiding a battle with men who had so recently been counted as allies, he extended the deadline to 17:30.

While Holland was talking to Gensoul, Somerville received a warning from the Admiralty that French reinforcements were en route. Somerville immediately sent Gensoul a message informing him that his ships would be sunk if none of the British proposals had been accepted by 17:30. This message was shown to Holland at 17:15, who sent a message to Somerville with some little progress, hoping to avoid conflict.

It was not to be. Holland left *Dunkerque*, the French flagship, at 17:25, and at 17:54 the British fleet fired the first shots. They were stationed to the north-west to reduce the possibility of misses hitting the town. The battleship

Bretagne suffered a magazine explosion and sank, taking 977 crew with her. *Provence*, *Dunkerque*, and the destroyer *Mogador* were damaged and run aground. *Strasbourg* and four destroyers managed to get to the open sea. They were attacked by Swordfish aircraft from Ark Royal, but to little effect. The British pursued them until 20:20, and Swordfish attacked them again at 20:55.

A British submarine sank the French gunboat *Rigault de Genouilly* the following day, and on 8th July, Swordfish launched a torpedo attack against *Dunkerque* and inflicted serious damage. On the same day, and also part of Operation Catapult, HMS *Hermes* mounted an airborne attack against the battleship *Richelieu* at Dakar, causing serious damage.

Operation Catapult resulted in the deaths of around 1,300 Frenchmen. One French battleship was sunk and two damaged. Three destroyers were damaged and one grounded. British losses were two dead and six aircraft destroyed. Public attitudes in Britain regarding the action were positive. The Ministry of Information reported "widespread approval" and a feeling that "no other course was possible"[1]. This soon hardened into anti-French attitudes, and feelings that Britain and France had never really been friends in the first place[2].

Admiral Gensoul had warned that shots fired against them would put "the whole French fleet against Great Britain", and he was not wrong. Anglo-French relations, already strained, sank even lower.

The Vichy government distrusted Britain and suspected her motives, believing that the British wanted to expand their empire at the expense of the French. France had already lost control of some parts of her empire to Japan and the Free French, and they hated the idea of losing more to Britain.

There is no evidence to suggest that Britain did wish to expand her empire at Vichy's expense, but the suspicion and fear were very real. Combined with a belief that Germany would ultimately win the war, and a deep-seated bitterness over the defeat of France and the attacks of Operation Catapult, they help to explain Vichy's belligerent attitude towards Britain.

The September 1940 battle at Dakar and the 1941 campaign in Syria and Lebanon hardened the Vichy attitude against Britain. At Dakar, de Gaulle hoped that he would be welcomed with open arms, but approaches were rebuffed and the Allies were defeated in the subsequent battle. In 1941 the British led an invasion of Syria and Lebanon, both of which were under Vichy control, in order to prevent Germany using the area as a base for attacks on Egypt.

2

CONCERNS ABOUT MADAGASCAR

When France first fell, the governor of Madagascar, Jules Marcel de Coppet, made a radio broadcast that appeared to favour de Gaulle over Vichy. News of the attack at Mers El Kébir gave him pause, but he failed to take decisive action. A distrustful Vichy replaced him with Léon Cayla, who remained as governor until ill health forced him to retire in April 1941. Cayla was succeeded by Armand Annet, a man loyal to Pétain.

Although Germany had designs on Madagascar, British concerns around the island centred on Japan. Even before the Japanese attack on Pearl Harbor, they were concerned that Japan would demand bases in Madagascar from Vichy France. Vichy had already conceded bases in French Indochina, and the British didn't believe they could refuse any further demands. There was a large natural harbour at Diego Suarez on the north of the island. The French had modernised the port and it had a dry dock large enough to hold a ship with a displacement of up to 26,000 tons. The base was well defended, with a large garrison and coastal batteries covering the seaward approach.

SOE (the Special Operations Executive) had an agent named Percy Mayer on the island, operating under the codename Carson and also referred to in official documents as DZ/6. His initial instructions were to encourage any opposition to Vichy, as the British hoped that the island's population could be brought over to the Allied cause. It soon became apparent that this was not feasible. Still, Mayer made efforts to recruit more agents. His wife, Berthe Mayer, helped with his SOE work under the designation DZ/60, and often operated the radio transmitter. At the end of October 1941, while Percy was in South Africa, she sent a signal about the movement of five Vichy merchant ships, totalling 40,000 tons. This signal led to their capture by the Royal Navy in early November. The director of Naval Intelligence, Admiral Godfrey, wrote a personal letter of gratitude to SOE for them to forward to Berthe Mayer, describing her work as "a very fine show indeed"[1].

In November 1941, the Joint Planning Staff were instructed to draw up plans for taking the north of the island. They invited SOE to a planning meeting, where their representative gained the impression that an action was likely in three or four months' time. The next day the Chiefs of Staff, obviously valuing the potential SOE contribution, requested that SOE "press on with the perfection of their Madagascar organisation"[2].

Three plans were drawn up, two of which required ships to steam directly into the port at Diego Suarez. The third, which was adopted, called for a land invasion some distance away from the port, and a subsequent land-based attack. This was named Operation Bonus, and over the next few weeks, detailed plans were drawn up and troops were assigned to the operation.

Percy Mayer thought it might be possible to bribe the senior French naval officer on Madagascar, Captain Maerten, into surrendering Diego Suarez to the British. Having obtained permission to try, he made an approach in late December 1941. Maerten rebuffed Mayer's approach, but did not report it to the authorities. Mayer continued his work for SOE, recruiting agents in various parts of the island.

SOE increased the size and effectiveness of their East African mission. It had previously faced opposition from other government departments, but that changed after Japan entered the war. They were able to set up a headquarters in Durban and base representatives in Portuguese East Africa. They acquired a schooner named *Lindi*, which was used to make covert voyages between Madagascar and Dar es Salaam in Tanganyika.

After the Japanese attack on Pearl Harbor, the British had other concerns. Churchill worried that the Japanese would demand the use of naval bases on Madagascar. This would allow their navy to roam the Indian Ocean, causing havoc among convoys bound for India and Burma. Convoys travelling from Britain to the Far East often sailed around the horn of Africa in order to avoid the war-torn Mediterranean. These convoys passed close by Madagascar, making them vulnerable to ships or submarines based there.

Churchill wasn't the only one to have seen these disturbing possibilities. On 16th December 1941, de Gaulle wrote to Churchill, urging a joint British and Free French operation to take the island. De Gaulle assured Churchill that "a very large proportion of the population of Madagascar is faithful to France and at the same time (indeed for that very reason) anxious to aid the Allied cause."[3] Although nobody realised it at the time, his confidence was misplaced.

Field Marshal Jan Smuts, the South African prime minister, was also concerned. He wrote to Churchill:

> "I look upon Madagascar as the key to the safety of the Indian Ocean, and it may play the same important part in endangering our security there that Indochina has played in Vichy and Japanese hands. All our communications with our various war fronts and the Empire in the East may be involved."[4]

Churchill accepted military advice that Madagascar was a low priority, although he still had concerns. Operation Bonus was officially cancelled at the end of January 1942.

In February 1942, de Gaulle wrote to Churchill once more about Madagascar, and proposed a plan for Free French forces to take the island with British air and naval support. The American Joint Chiefs of Staff were keen to ensure that the Japanese could not use Diego Suarez, and Churchill was still worried about Madagascar. However, the British Chiefs of Staff opposed any action there, saying that a large British force would be required, and that such forces would better serve the war effort in India, Ceylon, or the Indian Ocean.

The Chiefs of Staff considered Ceylon to be the most pressing issue, and Churchill eventually agreed. Still concerned about Madagascar, he insisted that some planning was carried out. If any action was to be taken, however, the ground forces would be made up entirely of

Free French or British Empire troops. He would not coun-
tenance a joint force, because of the problems that such a
force had faced at Dakar.

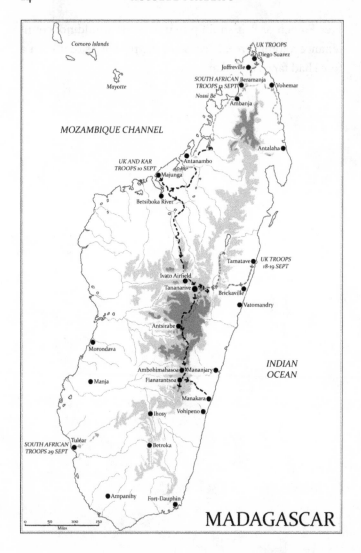

3

PLANNING

In March 1942, Admiral Raeder, the head of the German navy, reported that the Japanese Navy was planning to establish bases in Madagascar, though Hitler doubted that the French would agree to it. The Germans asked the Japanese to clarify their intentions, and the Americans intercepted and decoded these signals. The Japanese navy had an aircraft carrier task force in the eastern Indian Ocean, which seemed well placed to establish bases on the island. The prospect of the Germans and Japanese cooperating in this way changed attitudes among the Allies. On 12th March, the war cabinet agreed to an operation to take the northern part of Madagascar, now named Operation Ironclad. Churchill informed Smuts of the decision on 24th March 1942.

Roosevelt was determined that American forces would not be involved in the operation. He considered it important for the US to maintain diplomatic relations with Vichy France. However, on 29th March he agreed to deliver a note to the Vichy government on the day of the invasion. This note would explain the purpose of the inva-

sion and assure the French that the island would be
returned to French control once the war had been won.
The Allies hoped that this demonstration of American
support for the action would minimise any belligerent
reaction from Vichy.

Ironclad was going to involve a significant naval force.
The British navy in the Far East was too thinly stretched
to provide the ships, and so Force H, based at Gibraltar,
was assigned. Churchill wrote to President Roosevelt to
request an American force to be sent to Gibraltar to
relieve Force H. Roosevelt did not want to station American ships at Gibraltar, but he offered to take over all
escort duties in the North Atlantic or to send ships to reinforce the Royal Navy's Home Fleet. The latter offer was
taken up, and so the US dispatched two battleships, one
aircraft carrier, two cruisers, and a squadron of destroyers
to Britain.

The naval force for Operation Ironclad was designated
Force F. This would consist of the battleship *Malaya*,
aircraft carriers *Eagle* and *Hermes*, cruisers *Hermione* and
Devonshire, eleven destroyers, six corvettes, a flotilla of
minesweepers, two Fleet Auxiliaries, and the hospital ship
Atlantis. *Hermes* was sunk on 9th April, so HMS
Indomitable took her place. HMS *Illustrious* stood in for
HMS *Eagle*, which required repairs.

Strict secrecy surrounded the planning for Ironclad, to
stop the Japanese pre-empting the British invasion with
one of their own. This also avoided the possibility of
Vichy troops and/or supplies being sent from Dakar to
reinforce Madagascar. Although the British didn't know it,
the Germans had concluded that French security could
not be trusted after Vichy merchant ships were captured

in November 1941. As a result, they had forbidden any Vichy reinforcements being sent to the Indian Ocean.

Two units were assigned to the operation, 29th Independent Infantry Brigade and Number 5 (Army) Commando. Both of these units had trained in opposed amphibious landings, and were already assault loaded onto transport ships in preparation for an exercise. The 5th Infantry Division, which had been intended to sail for India, added its 17th Brigade to the operation. Once the north of the island had been taken, this brigade would be replaced by African units, and it would then continue on to India.

29th Independent Infantry Brigade sacrificed some of its motor transport to make room for an armoured unit. This was a composite squadron made up of two half squadrons from B and C Special Service Squadrons, equipped with Valentine infantry tanks and Tetrarch light tanks respectively. The Valentines were split into a troop of three under Lieutenant Heywood and a troop of two under Lieutenant Whitaker. The squadron commander, Major J.E.S. Simon, was in the remaining Valentine. The Tetrarchs were organised the same way: a troop of three tanks under Lieutenant Carlisle, a troop of two under Lieutenant Astle, and the squadron second-in-command, Captain Peter Llewellyn Palmer, in the last Tetrarch. Artillery reinforcements were provided in the shape of 455 Independent Light Battery, Royal Artillery with four 3.7" howitzers and two 25-pounders, and 145 Light Anti-Aircraft Troop, Royal Artillery with four 40mm Bofors guns.

Men of 29th Infantry Brigade training at Loch Fyne,
Argyllshire

The land forces, designated Force 121, were under the command of Major-General Sturges of the Royal Marines. The overall commander for Operation Ironclad was Rear-Admiral Syfret, who would be in charge during the voyage and assault. Subsequent operations on land would be under General Sturges.

17th Brigade's stores and vehicles had already sailed on 13th March 1942, with the rest of Force 121 sailing on 23rd March. Secrecy was still tight; the men of 29th Independent Infantry Brigade and 5 Commando were initially told that they were taking part in an exercise, and were only told the truth once they were at sea. Even then, they were not informed of their destination. Force F left Gibraltar under cover of darkness in the early hours of 1st April, heading south to rendezvous with the transport ships at Freetown in Sierra Leone.

Despite the long voyage and the threat of German U-boats, the transport ships arrived at Freetown without any losses. They had been attacked by one U-boat, but it was sunk by the escorts without any losses to the convoy. Force F was ordered to intercept the Vichy battleship *Richelieu* when she was reported to be leaving Dakar, but after three days of fruitless searching, they continued on to Freetown.

The officers were aware that such a long voyage in cramped conditions would be detrimental to morale and fitness. Marches, obstacle races, tugs of war, and other competitions were organised to alleviate these issues. The convoy of transport ships arrived at Freetown during the morning of 6th April 1942. The ships of Force F joined them three days later. In the interests of secrecy, the men were not allowed on shore, and false rumours were planted in the port about the convoy being headed for the Bay of Bengal.

The ships left Freetown on 10th and 11th April, heading for Durban in South Africa. On the 17th, General Sturges was informed that the 13th Brigade of the 5th Division had been assigned to the operation. This extra brigade, though, was strictly a reserve, to be committed only if necessary. If it was not required, it was to be sent on to India immediately.

Recent Japanese activity in the Indian Ocean had seemed to provide evidence that the taking of Madagascar was necessary. Carrier-based aircraft had attacked Ceylon twice, at Colombo on 5th April and the docks at Trincomalee on 9th April. The allies believed that at least five battleships and five aircraft carriers were operating in the Indian Ocean.

On 8th April, the Japanese naval attaché in Berlin, Vice Admiral Nomura, had met the German naval high command. He informed them that long-range submarines and auxiliary cruisers would operate off the east African coast from May to July. In Tokyo, the Japanese foreign minister had told the German ambassador that Japanese movements would satisfy the

German desire for a Japanese advance towards the Middle East.

The Japanese presence in the Indian Ocean made it implausible that the convoy was headed for the Bay of Bengal, so the cover story was changed. On 13th April, Syfret was informed of the new cover story, which named the Middle East as the final destination. To support this, the port of Alexandria made preparations to receive the convoy, and there was indiscreet talk of attacks on the Dodecanese Islands.

On 19th April, Syfret met Smuts in Cape Town. The South African prime minister offered the support of a squadron of the South African Air Force. Admiral Syfret appreciated the offer, but the distance made it difficult. It was agreed that fuel and ordnance for the squadron would be shipped with the convoy, and the squadron would fly to an airfield on Madagascar as soon as one had been captured.

On 20th April, Syfret left Cape Town to rendezvous with the rest of the force in Durban. HMS *Malaya* had been ordered to Freetown, so he transferred his flag to *Illustrious*. HMS *Ramillies* was en route to Durban from the Eastern Fleet to replace *Malaya*, and Syfret transferred his flag to her at Durban.

The whole force congregated at Durban on 22nd April, and South Africa broke off diplomatic relations with Vichy France on the same day. In order to keep the convoy's destination secret, a double bluff was prepared. A rumour was spread that the convoy was bound for Madagascar. Known enemy agents were fed the story that the Madagascar rumour was false, and that the real destination was Ceylon. Briefings were made and maps issued that reinforced the Ceylon story. Apparent lapses in secu-

rity allowed unauthorised personnel to see the maps,
leading to the news getting ashore.

A lot of work had to be done before the convoy left
Durban. Many of the cargoes had to be removed and
combat loaded. This placed the emphasis on unloading
combat supplies quickly and as needed, rather than the
more usual emphasis on efficient use of space. Troops
were exercised and drilled. Maintenance was carried out
on machines and vehicles. The plan was finalised and
orders were distributed. Admiral Somerville, Commander-in-Chief of the Eastern Fleet, arranged for HMS
Indomitable to join the naval forces. He also reported on
his plans to ensure that Japanese surface ships could not
interfere with the operation.

A new type of ship joined the force at Durban: the SS
Bachaquero. This was a tank landing ship, or LST. Back in
1940, Churchill, predicting the need for amphibious landings on enemy territory, had called for the development of
this type of vessel. Armed with three two-pounder pom-
pom guns, six 20mm Oerlikons, two smoke mortars, and
two Lewis machine guns, she carried two LCMs (Landing
Craft, Mechanised). She could carry her load across
oceans, then either dispatch her cargo on the LCMs or
beach herself, allowing her cargo to drive straight off and
onto the beach. This would be the first operational use of
this new type of ship, whose existence was a closely
guarded secret.

By this time, Percy Mayer had provided the force
commanders with remarkably detailed intelligence about
the forces and political situation on the island. He had
managed to get on board the French submarine *Bévéziers*,
and persuaded a French sergeant to give him a guided
tour of the defences at Courrier Bay in the north. As the

day of the landing approached, Mayer and his wife sent frequent updates. Mayer would drive around the area, meeting French commanders and finding out exactly where troops were positioned. One message indicated that the island of Nossi Anambo, on the approach to the landing area, was not in the location the Royal Navy's charts showed. Had it not been corrected, this mistake could have led to the fleet approaching the wrong part of the island. Admiral Syfret later commented that Mayer's intelligence reports had been "most valuable"[1].

The ships left on 25th and 28th April 1942. Even as they sailed to Madagascar, there was the possibility of cancellation. General Alan Brooke, who had always opposed the plan, expressed his concerns to Churchill on 1st May, but the prime minister was not to be dissuaded. On the same day, the fleet received their final confirmation from London that the invasion was to go ahead, and the true destination was broadcast to each ship's company.

Smuts had long since pressed for action against Madagascar and was keen that the whole island should be taken. Churchill still believed that securing the northern part of the island, particularly the port at Diego Suarez, would be sufficient. He wrote to General Wavell in India, telling him they hoped to minimise the time taken in securing Diego Suarez by "the use of strong forces and severe, violent action."[2] Once this was done, the forces would move on to India. He expected the 5th Division to be with Wavell in May, followed by the 2nd Division in June.

The ships headed to Madagascar using the normal shipping lanes, as if they were heading to India or points further east. HMS *Indomitable* and two destroyers joined them on 3rd May, and they formed up for the final approach on the afternoon of the 4th. The French considered a night attack to be impossible, and so did not bother to defend against one. HMS *Hermione* set off on the 4th to sail around to Ambodivahibe Bay to the east of Diego Suarez, where she would mount a diversion.

The SOE schooner *Lindi*, captained by Lieutenant Aubrey Booker of the Royal Navy Voluntary Reserve, was stationed off the island of Nossi Anambo, displaying a light to guide the British ships. A full moon also helped. As the ships approached, the minesweepers worked, clearing a way for the others. Even the explosions of several mines did not alert the defenders to the pending assault. At 01:30 the assault ships anchored, and the first landing craft were launched an hour later. These carried men of 5 Commando and 2nd Battalion, East Lancashire Regiment.

According to General Alan Brooke, Churchill was elated and excited on the eve of the Madagascar invasion. After a long string of defeats and bad news, both Churchill and the British public longed for a victory.

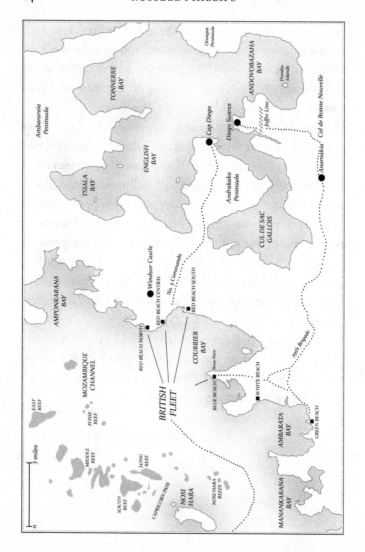

4

OPERATION IRONCLAD

On the night of 4th/5th May 1942, Percy Mayer cut the telephone cable that connected the artillery battery covering the landing beaches on Courrier Bay with the headquarters at Diego Suarez. Mayer then waited for the landings to take place, intending to pass on some final information that he had been unable to transmit by radio. Not knowing the time of the landings, he waited until 02:40 before returning to Diego Suarez, assuming the landings had been postponed.

In Diego Suarez the police acted on a tip-off and arrested him. He managed to rip up the intelligence notes that he was carrying, but the police were able to reconstruct them. The authorities charged him with espionage and pronounced a death sentence. By this time, the attack on the island had begun.

At 04:30 on 5th May, HMS *Hermione* started a bombardment off Ambodivahibe Bay, a potential landing site on the east of the island. She fired star and smoke shells, made a smoke screen, and dropped burning tar barrels to give the impression of an invasion convoy. To enhance the deception, three Swordfish aircraft dropped eighteen dummy paratroopers inland, close to a police post north of Col de la Herte. *Hermione* later tried to engage the shore batteries at Cap Miné, but they had a greater range than her guns and she was forced to withdraw.

Hermione's deception efforts, paired with Mayer's espionage, paid dividends. The artillery commander at Windsor Castle could not call Colonel Claerebout at Diego Suarez, so the latter believed that the invasion was indeed coming from the east. He therefore sent his only motorised force, a reconnaissance unit, to deal with the supposed paratroopers.

The British still held out some hope that they could take the island without bloodshed. To this end, aircraft dropped leaflets on Diego Suarez, asking the defenders not to oppose the invasion. The leaflets tried to explain why the island was being invaded and offered reassurances that it would be returned to French control once the war was won. It didn't work — the French responded that the garrison would "defend to the last"[1]. Admiral Syfret was not happy about the leaflet drops, later saying that they were useless and dangerous. Conversely, Annet claimed that they would have been better received if they had not arrived after bombing attacks that killed French sailors.

Bombing of artillery batteries and ships in Diego Suarez harbour accompanied the leaflet drops, and this hardened feeling against the Allies. All the aircraft involved in this operation flew around the island before approaching from the east, reinforcing the deception that the attack was being mounted from that direction.

5 Commando and B Company of 2nd Battalion East Lancashire Regiment started landing on Red Beach in Courrier Bay at about 04:30 on 5th May. Intelligence believed that there were two artillery batteries, each of four guns, positioned to fire on Red Beach. The commandoes had been given the task of putting these guns out of action. In fact, there was only one battery, and Percy Mayer's work cutting telephone cables meant that it could not communicate with the rest of the forces on the island.

The commandoes reached the guns to discover that they were not manned. They removed the breech blocks and moved them away in case of counter-attack. Two French officers saw them and put up a fight, wounding one British soldier before being killed. The commandoes moved onto the barracks, capturing the occupants, many of whom were still asleep as they arrived.

3 Troop of 5 Commando were left to guard the guns and prisoners, and at 05:30 a detachment from 3 Troop began an attack on the battery's observation post. This was located in a strong position on a promontory named Windsor Castle. At 06:00, the post appeared to surrender, but when an officer went forward to take the surrender, he was shot and wounded. Aircraft from the fleet bombed and strafed the position later in the morning, but the defenders, armed with small arms and a 60mm mortar, refused to budge.

Meanwhile, 4 and 5 Troops of 5 Commando had been searching for the second battery that intelligence had reported. Having decided that intelligence had been mistaken, they met 6 Troop at the beach. At 06:05 these three troops set off to rendezvous with 1 and 2 Troops, HQ Troop, B Company of 2nd Battalion East Lancashire Regiment, and two Universal Carriers. They made the rendezvous at 09:00, and the advance on Cap Diego began.

Initially, the advance came across no organised resistance, encountering only small parties that quickly surrendered. They met the first organised resistance at 12:30, when the Universal Carriers, which were leading the column, came across prepared positions including a pair of 65mm field guns. A brief fight ensued before the French surrendered with the loss of one officer and twelve men. The British suffered no losses.

As the advance continued, there was some desultory sniper fire. The Universal Carriers entered Cap Diego at 14:30, accompanied by 5 Troop and 6 Troop. The defenders surrendered within half an hour. The commandoes took around two hundred Malagasy and twenty-three European prisoners.

Back at Windsor Castle, gunfire support was requested from *Devonshire* at 11:26. The captain launched his Walrus sea plane instead. This made several bombing runs and was later joined by Sea Hurricanes and Albacores. The air attacks had little impact on the defenders' resolve, however.

At 14:00 the 2nd Battalion Royal Scots Fusiliers had taken over guard duties from 3 Troop of 5 Commando. At 15:00, naval gunfire against Windsor Castle was requested, and *Laforey* opened fire at 15:26. A white flag appeared, but as the commandoes went forward to take the surrender, grenades were thrown at them, wounding their commander. Three ships now fired on the position, but despite a direct hit on the living quarters, the defenders held firm.

At 16:00, 3 Troop moved off to join the rest of 5 Commando at Cap Diego, leaving the Royal Scots Fusiliers to continue the fight against the Windsor Castle garrison. The next morning, the 2nd Battalion Royal Inniskilling Fusiliers took over from the Royal Scots Fusiliers, who had been ordered to advance to Con Barriquand.

The Royal Scots Fusiliers and Royal Welch Fusiliers had landed on Green Beach that morning, while the East Lancashire Regiment landed on Blue Beach. The East Lancashires faced opposition from around fifty Senegalese infantry with machine guns. The Senegalese fired at the landing craft as they approached the beach. Lifeboats from HMS *Royal Ulsterman* were also used in the landing. These had Bren guns in the bows, allowing them to return fire.

Percy Mayer had warned of these defending troops, and so plans had been made. After landing, one company of the Royal Welch Fusiliers headed north towards Basse Point, behind Blue Beach. The Senegalese, outnumbered and facing attack from two directions, retreated in disorder. Their huts were burned to ensure that nobody was left hiding in them. Once this was done, all the beaches were secured.

A Valentine tank of B Special Service Squadron being unloaded from LST Bachaquero at Freetown, Sierra Leone

The tank landing ship HMS *Bachaquero* moved
towards Blue Beach at around 06:00, but was delayed
when more mines were found. Once the mines had been
cleared, it was discovered that beach conditions made it
impossible for the ship to land and it would have to
unload its cargo by landing craft, negating some of the
advantages of such a specialised ship. Before this
unloading began, news came that Red Beach had a suitable landing place. *Bachaquero* moved north, but
grounded on a sandbank, with deep water between her
and the beach. A wooden jetty was built to link her to the
beach, which allowed three Universal Carriers to land, but
other vehicles failed to make it and had to be pulled onto
shore by soldiers pulling on ropes.

The tanks of B and C Special Service Squadrons had
not been carried on HMS *Bachaquero*, and were all landed
by Tank Landing Craft (LCT) by 10:00.

At around midday, the minesweeper *Auricula* hit a
mine. Her crew were safely taken off, and although she
did not sink, she was too badly damaged to be taken
under tow. She was left floating at anchor. A pair of
French fighters conducted strafing attacks on the beaches
twice during the afternoon, but no casualties were
recorded.

By 17:15 the tide had risen to the point where no more
vehicles could be landed unless *Bachaquero* was able to
land higher on the beach. Her captain, Lieutenant
Commander McMullan, had her taken out about one and
a half kilometres, then charged at full speed towards the
beach. She crashed through the sandbank, then cut the
engines as she approached the beach. *Bachaquero* landed
successfully, and the rest of her cargo was quickly
unloaded. By 19:00 she was fully unloaded and able to

leave the beach. Teething issues notwithstanding, she had proved the usefulness of the LST concept.

When darkness fell around 18:00, some troops and equipment were still on board ships, but disembarkation was halted until 22:30, when there was sufficient moonlight. The landings continued throughout the night, with companies of infantry marching towards Diego Suarez as soon as they were formed up. They passed wounded men heading in the opposite direction, bound for the hospital ship *Atlantis*, moored in Courrier Bay.

5

ADVANCE TO DIEGO SUAREZ,
5TH MAY

Six Swordfish aircraft flown from *Illustrious* approached Diego Suarez Bay at around 05:00 on 5th May. Several ships were in the bay, along with the submarine *Bévéziers*, which had crippled the British battleship *Resolution* at Dakar. All six Swordfish launched torpedoes at the sloop *D'Entrecasteaux*. They all missed their target, but one passed underneath and struck the auxiliary cruiser *Bougainville*, which had just got under way. She started to sink, but the crew continued to fire at the attackers until she was hit a second time.

A second wave of aircraft, carrying depth charges, attacked and sank *Bévéziers* as she tried to move away from the jetty. The surviving crew from *Bougainville* and *Bévéziers* joined the infantry defending the town.

A third wave of aircraft dropped leaflets over Diego Suarez before bombing the battery at Lazaret Point, then attacked *D'Entrecasteaux*, setting it on fire; it ran aground in Andohazampo Cove. By this time, the French gunners were well prepared, and the aircraft were subjected to heavy anti-aircraft fire. The commander of the Cap Diego battery even rowed out into the bay to better judge the effectiveness of his guns' fire.

Swordfish attacked *D'Entrecasteaux* again at 15:00, with bombs and machine gun fire. The ship was seriously damaged, but three of the attacking aircraft were hit, two of them being out of action for several days.

D'Entrecasteaux after the battle for Diego Suarez

To the south of Diego Suarez was Arrachart airfield, which was attacked first by Albacores flown from *Indomitable*. They first dropped leaflets, and then five minutes later they dropped bombs and incendiaries. Eight Sea Hurricanes, also from *Indomitable*, followed them, with instructions to destroy "anything and everything of military importance left on the aerodrome". Two Potez 63 bombers, two Potez 25 biplanes, five Morane-Saulnier 406 fighters, and one civilian aircraft were destroyed in the attack. In addition, some hangars were damaged and the detachment commander was killed.

Indomitable also launched three Fulmar IIs to attack Vohemar aerodrome, 115km to the south of Arrachart. This was to prevent French aircraft based at Tananarive using it as a forward base.

Once they were ashore, the 1st Battalion Royal Scots Fusiliers and 2nd Battalion Royal Welch Fusiliers moved through the swamps surrounding the beaches to start the advance inland. At 06:37, they met on a poorly maintained road that led to the main Diego Suarez–Arrachart road. The Royal Welch Fusiliers had arrived first, and so they were given the mission of advancing on Diego Suarez. The Scots, as the later arrivals, were to take Arrachart airfield.

Fifteen minutes later, at Mangorky, motorbikes and Universal Carriers caught up with 2nd Battalion Royal Welch Fusiliers and took the lead. Most of 2nd Battalion's motor transport was still on board ship, and so the men had to march carrying their equipment. The locals seemed unconcerned, and the advance continued without incident until they reached the village of Anamakia. Here, at about 08:15, one of the Universal Carriers captured a French naval officer, named Capitaine Yvernat, and three ratings. The British still held out some slim hope that they could take the island without force, and so Yvernat was allowed to go to Diego Suarez in his own car, to deliver a letter from Admiral Syfret to the French commander, Colonel Claerebout. The letter's message was much the same as the leaflets that were dropped on Diego Suarez, containing assurances that the island would remain French.

Yvernat reached Diego Suarez at about 09:00. The letter was ignored, but Yvernat, who had been able to observe some of the British forces, was able to give some indication of the size and composition of the force advancing on Diego Suarez. That the British were advancing in that direction was not a great surprise to Claerebout, who had sent Yvernat to investigate why the battery at Windsor Castle had gone silent. In addition, the commander of the Windsor Castle battery had sent runners at 06:30 and 06:45. Yvernat's report confirmed that this was the main effort, however, rather than the commandoes advancing on Cap Diego.

A company of Senegalese light infantry was quickly sent to take up prepared positions at a ridge named Col de

Bonne Nouvelle to delay the advancing force. Three companies of infantry were ordered to man the Joffre Line, a set of defensive positions at the base of the peninsula.

The leading British Universal Carriers arrived at Col de Bonne Nouvelle at 11:15 and suffered the first casualty of the action when the driver of Brigadier Festing's vehicle was shot in the hand. Festing immediately realised that a frontal assault would be costly, and so ordered two companies to the flanks and called for armoured support from the tank squadron. He also warned the 1st Battalion Royal Scots Fusiliers, who had started their march on Arrachart airfield, that their assistance might be required. The Scots therefore started to move north towards the fight.

As soon as two Valentine and one Tetrarch tank had landed, they were sent forward to help the infantry, under the command of Major Simon. They drove towards the ridge, but were unable to elevate their armament high enough to engage the defenders effectively. Two 3.7" howitzers of 455 Light Battery Royal Artillery had arrived by this time, and they began shelling the positions as the tanks advanced.

The Royal Welch Fusiliers continued to take casualties from the Senegalese, including two officers killed by snipers. By 14:00, lead elements of the 2nd Battalion South Lancashire Regiment had reached the col and were available to assist in the attack. Constant shelling from the artillery convinced the defenders to leave their positions in favour of a trench to the rear. Covered by the artillery and supported by the South Lancashires, the Fusiliers took the hill with a bayonet charge at 15:00.

Thirty of the defenders were killed, and almost all of

those who were taken prisoner were wounded. It was obvious to Brigadier Festing that Diego Suarez would not surrender without a fight. As well as the two officers killed, a number of British enlisted men were wounded, and 2nd Battalion Royal Welch Fusiliers were exhausted. The 1st Battalion Royal Scots Fusiliers resumed the advance at 15:15, with Universal Carriers leading the way. The Royal Welch Fusiliers were allowed some time to rest before following.

6

ATTACK ON DIEGO SUAREZ, 5TH MAY

While the infantry dealt with the prisoners, the tanks had already been ordered ahead to the town. At this point in the war, the British army had not fully appreciated the lesson that tanks should operate as part of a combined force, with infantry and artillery. Indeed, tanks were seen as self-sufficient, and the armoured charge was still included in training drills.[1]

By now, a troop of three Tetrarchs had been sent on from the landing beach. One of the extra tanks had thrown a track in soft sand[2], so five tanks (two Valentines and three Tetrarchs) went on to Diego Suarez. The Valentines took the lead and stayed about four hundred metres ahead of the lighter Tetrarchs. The British didn't believe that the French forces on Madagascar had any weapons capable of penetrating the heavy armour of the Valentine infantry tanks.

The attackers didn't know it, but Diego Suarez had a defensive line about five and a half kilometres long. There was a fort at each end of the line, with a trench system running the length of it. There were pillboxes, machine gun posts, 75mm gun emplacements, and mortar pits at intervals along the line. An anti-tank ditch was positioned about 1,400 metres ahead of the line, and there were several mobile 75mm guns, pulled by bullocks.

These defences were known as the "Joffre Line", and were originally created by General Joffre in 1909, when he was the fortress commander. They were well camouflaged, and had not been spotted by the reconnaissance flights flown by the South African Air Force. Percy Mayer had sent information about Diego Suarez's defences to East Africa Command HQ in Nairobi, but for some reason the information had not been passed on to the commanders of Operation Ironclad. The defences were marked "Ouvrage" on the British commanders' maps. "Ouvrage" translates literally to "work" and the British thought it indicated a factory or something similar, whereas it actually indicated "defensive works".

A Tetrarch tank, of the type used by C Special Service Squadron on Madagascar

The tanks followed the road to Diego Suarez and found themselves on a flat plain with the town and its defences ahead. As they approached the town, 75mm guns opened fire on the Valentines. Still thinking that their armour was proof against the French weapons, the tanks continued. The leading Valentine was hit and its driver killed, then further hits jammed the turret mechanism. The commander and gunner bailed out; the gunner was wounded by machine gun fire as they did so.

The second Valentine also took fire. Its turret jammed and the gear change mechanism was damaged, slowing but not stopping it. Major Simon, in command, ordered the crew to bail out. The driver, suffering somewhat from concussion, fell in front of the still-moving tank, which rolled over him and killed him.

Two of the three Tetrarchs were also hit. Lieutenant Astle had managed to stop his in some dead ground, and he crawled forward to find out if he could assist the survivors. He found four men capable of fighting, and four wounded. Major Simon ordered him to return to Brigade headquarters and report on the situation. During his return journey, Astle's tank encountered a lorry of Senegalese troops apparently heading to reinforce Col de Bonne Nouvelle. He destroyed the lorry, killing and capturing the infantry.

Sergeant Grime, a gunner from one of the Valentines, made repeated journeys under fire to recover weapons, ammunition, water, and first aid equipment from the damaged tanks. After a while, a motorbike arrived with a liaison officer, who took the most badly burnt man back to Brigade headquarters. Major Simon was convinced that this action saved the man's life.

The tank crews hid in the long pampas grass as Senegalese infantry searched for them and attacked with bayonets. Two attacks were beaten off, but at 15:45, with ammunition running very low, Second Lieutenant Whitaker was fatally wounded in a hand-to-hand fight.

The rest of the British tankers were captured, and would have been killed but for the intervention of a French officer.

Sergeant Grime was awarded the Distinguished Conduct Medal (DCM) for his part in the action. His citation notes that he was "consistently cheerful and determined, and behaved with the utmost contempt of danger."[3]

By 17:00 the infantry had moved up behind a ridge some distance from the Joffre Line defences. Lieutenant Astle's Tetrarch was with them, and had been reinforced by four Valentines and two more Tetrarchs. These seven tanks were all that remained of the original twelve tanks, one Tetrarch having got stuck on the beach when salt water got into its electrical circuits.

With Major Simon captured, Captain Palmer took over command of the tank squadron. He called a quick conference, where it was decided that the tanks would make a head-on charge at full speed, in the hope of taking the gunners by surprise. Palmer would take the lead in a Valentine, with the other tanks in an arrowhead formation behind.

This attack began at 17:30, with mortars laying a smoke screen. It didn't go well. Sergeant Clegg, commanding a Tetrarch tank, described it as a "re-run of Balaclava". As soon as they were in the open, they started taking heavy fire. One Valentine was hit, and the wounded crew managed to bail out and find cover. Palmer's tank was hit, and the crew ran for cover. The driver fell and Palmer, himself wounded, went back to help him. Just as Palmer reached the driver, a high explosive shell landed directly on them, killing them both. Brigadier Festing recommended Palmer for the Victoria Cross. This was denied, but he was awarded a posthumous Military Cross. The surviving two Valentines and three Tetrarchs kept firing on the defences for as long as there was sufficient light for them to do so.

C Company of the 1st Battalion Royal Scots Fusiliers attacked with the tanks, closely supported by D Company. One platoon was to the left of the road, the other two to the right. Meanwhile, B Company pushed to the right in an effort to outflank the defenders. They were followed by A Company, but they both returned to their starting positions as it got dark. The two platoons of D Company to the right of the road managed to reach the anti-tank ditch, but could not get any further. The platoon to the left didn't even get that far. Heavy fire from machine guns and snipers stopped their advance after one hundred metres.

The British took advantage of darkness to pause and regroup. Brigadier Festing began work on a plan for a night attack.

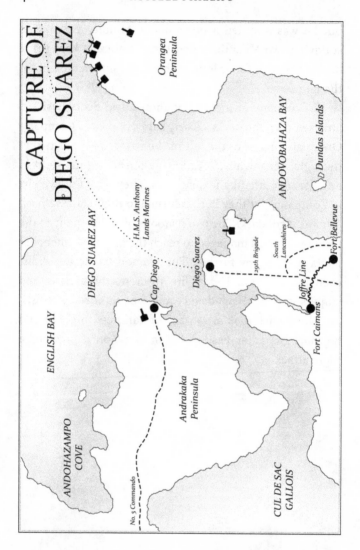

CAPTURE OF
DIEGO SUAREZ

Orangea Peninsula

ANDOVOBAHAZA BAY

Dundas Islands

DIEGO SUAREZ BAY

H.M.S. Anthony
Lands Marines

Diego Suarez

129th Brigade

South
Lancashires

Joffre Line

Fort Bellevue

Fort Caimans

Cap Diego

ENGLISH BAY

ANDOHAZAMPO
COVE

Andrakaka
Peninsula

CUL DE SAC
GALLOIS

No. 5 Commando

7

DIEGO SUAREZ, 6TH MAY

By now, the 2nd Battalion of the South Lancashire Regiment had landed and started their march towards Diego Suarez. They encountered sniping and machine gun fire at Con Barriquand, leading to a delay and a few casualties. By the evening, they were with the other British forces ahead of the Joffre Line.

The South Lancashires' role in the night attack was to move east at 02:00 on 6th May, around the French flank and to their rear. The South Lancashires would then attack from the French rear as the 1st Royal Scots Fusiliers and 2nd Battalion East Lancashire Regiment attacked the front. The attack would be preceded by air strikes from Swordfish and Albacores launched from the aircraft carriers, and supported by 3.7" howitzers from the 455 Light Battery, Royal Artillery.

The South Lancashires set off on time at 02:00 in three columns, fifty metres apart. The difficult terrain and darkness meant that each company had to stop frequently in order to maintain unit cohesion, so progress was slow.

On reaching the coast, they turned north in two

columns. The left column, in relatively open terrain, was able to advance deployed, while the right column was in single file. The right column encountered two sentries, who were killed before they could raise the alarm. By 05:30, they still hadn't reached their attack start point at the cemetery. One platoon from B Company, which should have been in the right column, was actually with D Company in the left column. A Company, also of the right column, had lost two platoons which were trying to catch up.

Between 04:00 and 05:00, the 1st Battalion Royal Scots Fusiliers and 2nd Battalion Royal Welch Fusiliers sent out fighting patrols to distract the French, so that they would not notice the South Lancashires to their flank and rear.

At 05:00 Swordfish and Albacore aircraft bombed the Joffre Line. The positions were very well camouflaged and they had difficulty locating their targets. At 05:30 they were followed by Martlet fighters which strafed the lines and shot down two French Potez 63 light bombers.

The South Lancashires started operations at 05:30, as planned. They hadn't been able to get to their intended start positions, but they did manage to cause considerable difficulties for the French. B Company captured two machine gun posts and the barracks at Ano Bozaka, taking thirty prisoners. Unable to continue with the original plan, the company was ordered to split into guerrilla groups of section strength and cause as much damage as possible. Some of these bands captured and stampeded pack horses and mules used to move the French 75mm guns, denying them to the French and adding to the confusion. Some managed to get within range of the French front lines and open fire on them. These guerrilla bands continued harassing the French throughout the day.

The South Lancashires' forward HQ and A Company (minus two platoons that were heavily engaged) moved into the village south of Diego Suarez. There they cut telephone wires and ambushed vehicles, before capturing the radio transmission station at 07:00. They remained there, fighting off counter-attacks, making repeated failed attempts to contact Brigade headquarters by radio, and suffering artillery fire and bombing attacks from the British. At dusk, they made their way back to the Brigade's positions.

C and D Companies, which had been in the left column, captured the reservoir, then captured several posts and took a number of prisoners. Attacks were made against Fort Bellevue, but they were repulsed. An enterprising lieutenant led a patrol to within fifty metres of the fort without being seen, then demanded the fort's surrender. The defenders refused to surrender, but allowed the patrol to retreat unmolested. After dark, D Company withdrew, but C Company remained at the reservoir.

The plan was that 5 Commando would cross from Cap Diego to Diego Suarez to assist in the attack, but they failed to do so. There is some controversy over this. The official reason was that they couldn't find any boats, and the SOE officer assigned to 5 Commando reported that no orders were received until an hour before the assault, but he was sure that "an attempt would have been made without orders if boats had been available". However, officers in the unit later claimed that boats had been found, but the commanding officer would not issue the necessary orders. He was an alcoholic and, having been denied the chance to drink, couldn't bring himself to make a decision.

The sloop *D'Entrecasteaux*, grounded but still active, shelled 5 Commando and British vehicles in Cap Diego. Her fire was guided by a force of marines that she had landed, and who had recaptured some ground. Swordfish aircraft from *Indomitable* bombed her, but she only stopped firing after sustained shelling from the destroyer *Laforey*.

75mm gun emplacement on the Joffre Line

The frontal attack went in as planned, but soon faltered. The French 75mm guns and machine guns were well placed to give mutual covering fire, and there was little cover for the attacking infantry. The South Lancashires had been unable to contact Brigade HQ, so Sturges was unaware that they'd taken so many prisoners, or of the chaos that they were wreaking behind the French lines. Indeed, from his perspective, the attack appeared to be an almost complete failure. Some of the attackers were trapped in the anti-tank ditch, but most managed to return to their units during a lull later in the morning.

The attack could not be abandoned completely, however. Berthe Mayer had sent a radio message from

Tananarive, stating that forces were being assembled there for a move north to Diego Suarez, and the Vichy authorities had asked the Japanese to occupy the island to deny it to the British. Sturges' immediate concern, though, was that the forces at Camp d'Ambre near Joffreville might sever communications with the landing beaches. He needed to take Diego Suarez without delay, or be forced to fight on two fronts.

It was decided that another attack would be made that evening, by the newly-disembarked and still fresh 17th Brigade, supported by the 29th. The defenders were to be harassed for the rest of the day, by aircraft and by 25-pounders from the 9th Field Regiment, Royal Artillery. Zero hour was planned for 20:00. The British were also harassed, by sniper fire and occasional artillery fire.

The Vichy French government, having learned of the invasion, had cabled Governor Annet with instructions to resist "by every means and to the last cartridge." Admiral Darlan sent a separate message, in which he referred to the invasion as "highway robbery", and reminded Annet of the British "betrayal" at Dunkirk, and the attacks at Mers El Kébir, Dakar, and Syria.

Sturges rode a Universal Carrier to the landing beaches and arrived on *Ramillies* at around 14:00 on 6th May. He informed Syfret of the lack of progress, and that he intended to attack again that evening, after dark but before the moon rose at 23:00. Syfret offered help from the navy. The enemy positions were outside gun range, but aircraft could bomb the French positions until the attack began.

Sturges requested a force of twenty to thirty sailors to be landed on the Diego Suarez peninsula, behind the enemy rear. Syfret countered with an offer of fifty Royal

Marines, but he would need zero hour to be delayed until 20:30 to give him time to put a force together and sail the hundred and fifty kilometres to Diego Suarez. This was agreed, and Sturges also promised assistance from 5 Commando, if they were able to cross Port Nievre.

As Sturges headed back, a force of fifty Royal Marines from HMS *Ramillies* was assembled under Captain Price RM, and embarked upon the destroyer HMS *Anthony*. At 15:30, *Anthony* set off to Diego Suarez. Syfret was not happy. Sturges had left him with the impression that the night attack was unlikely to succeed. The initial landings had been made on the west coast to avoid the coastal gun batteries guarding Diego Suarez, and now *Anthony* would have to run that well-armed gauntlet. Syfret expected the Royal Marines to suffer around 60% casualties, and it seemed likely that *Anthony* would be sunk. It looked like the operation was going to turn into a long, drawn-out affair, the very thing they wanted to avoid. On top of this, two Vichy submarines were known to be in the area, and intelligence reports indicated that Japanese submarines were en route to the western half of the Indian Ocean.

Unbeknown to Admiral Syfret, things were starting to look up for the British. A battery of 25-pounders had been landed and had reinforced the artillery bombarding the French positions. Later in the afternoon, the commanding officer of the 2nd Battalion South Lancashire Regiment arrived back in British lines. The battalion had been thought lost, but their colonel was able to give a more accurate report of the havoc they had wrought behind the enemy lines.

When Brigadier Festing made a reconnaissance at 15:30, he saw signs that the French resolve was weakening. A fighting patrol of Universal Carriers found that they were able to penetrate further than had previously been possible. This was followed by a probe carried out by the tanks. One Valentine was disabled by artillery fire, but the remaining tanks discovered and fired upon a group of infantry in a sugarcane field. A later patrol from the Royal Scots Fusiliers captured fifty prisoners.

Meanwhile, many of the marines on *Anthony* were suffering from seasickness. They were used to life aboard a battleship which, being about twenty times heavier than a destroyer, gave a much smoother ride. At around 19:45 on the 6th, *Anthony* began approaching the entrance to Diego Suarez Bay, with the cruisers *Hermione* and *Devonshire* behind, ready to provide covering fire. It was now two hours after nightfall and in the darkness the entrance was barely visible, but *Anthony* went in at a speed of twenty-two knots. A shore-based searchlight picked up *Anthony* and the shore batteries opened fire. *Devonshire* and *Hermione* returned fire with their 8" guns, and *Anthony* opened fire with all of her own guns. The searchlight was extinguished, and *Anthony* was undamaged.

Aided by a hand-drawn map showing the positions of damaged ships, *Anthony* crossed the bay and headed to the main jetty, under machine gun fire from the jetty and the hill above. One enterprising artillery commander named Capitaine Clavel even had his men man-handle their 75mm gun onto the jetty, to fire at the destroyer at point-blank range. They managed to fire a single shot, but in the rush and confusion failed to hit the ship.[1]

Anthony overshot the jetty and had to back up. The marines climbed over the destroyer's depth charges to disembark over the stern. Once all the marines were off, the destroyer ran the gauntlet of the shore batteries once more. Remarkably, she made it out of the bay and back to the rest of the fleet intact. In Admiral Syfret's words, it was "a fine achievement brilliantly carried out".

The marines first rushed the 75mm gun that had fired on HMS *Anthony*, scattering its crew. They had been briefed to take the artillery commandant's house, but they weren't sure where it was. After some stumbling around, they managed to find it, and it was occupied without opposition. They started some fires in the area, and three sections were sent further down the road and came under fire from a barracks. The marines returned fire, and soon after, the artillery commandant walked out under a white flag and his surrender was taken. The commandant issued an order to his troops, and the marines were briefly concerned that they'd been tricked. They relaxed as it became clear that the order he'd issued was "cease fire".

The marines discovered that the barracks held around fifty British prisoners, mostly infantry but also some tank and air crew. There were enough captured French weapons to arm all the newly liberated prisoners, doubling the size of the force under Captain Price's command. The newly expanded force deployed to defend against any counter-attacks that the French might mount against them. Contrary to the expected near-suicidal nature of the marines' attack, none of them were killed, and only one was wounded, in a "rude but unimportant part of his anatomy"[2]. Captain Price RM and Lieutenant-Commander John Hodges, HMS *Anthony*'s skipper, were both awarded the Distinguished Service Order.

The artillery bombardment had little effect, but the South Lancashires' guerrilla actions had caused confusion and some loss of morale. The dark of the night also favoured the British, as much of the defensive fire was aimed too high. Nonetheless, the victory was hard won, with the British having to resort to bayonet charges. At 23:00, the leading units were past the Joffre Line and were north of the village of Antanambad. This was the cue for the reserve battalions to advance, and they moved through the French defences and onto Diego Suarez.

Some of the Royal Marines that were landed in Diego Suarez from HMS Anthony

There was some confusion in the town, but Colonel Claerebout, the commander of Diego Suarez, and Captain Maerten, the commander of the French navy in Madagascar, whom Mayer had earlier tried to bribe, were captured at about 01:00. Both Claerebout and Maerten insisted that they would only surrender to senior officers, and they finally surrendered to Brigadier Festing at 01:45 on 7th May. By 03:00, Diego Suarez was finally in British hands, but it took a few hours for the word to pass everywhere.

SOE officers attached to Festing's command soon discovered that Percy Mayer had been captured and sentenced to death for espionage. They immediately issued a warrant for his release, and were relieved when he arrived safely at the Brigadier's headquarters. The French authorities had been too preoccupied to carry out his sentence. The newly liberated Mayer stayed at the headquarters, acting as an advisor, where he was "of the utmost value".

8

JOFFRE LINE FORTS AND THE
ORANGEA PENINSULA

The forts on the Joffre Line were still manned and a threat, but were not a priority, given that they were isolated and surrounded. The powerful shore batteries on the Orangea Peninsula were another matter. British ships could not safely enter Diego Suarez Bay until they had been neutralised. General Sturges sent a message to Admiral Syfret at 03:13 on the morning of 7th May, requesting all available naval and air support for an attack on the Orangea peninsula at 09:00. The fleet moved eastward in order to be in position by daylight. The planned bombardment was put off until 10:00, with the land attack planned for 12:00.

During the night, the French submarine *Le Héros* returned from a convoy escort mission. She was attacked and sunk by the corvette HMS *Genista* and Swordfish from *Illustrious*. Around fifty survivors were later captured. At dawn, three French Morane-Saulnier 406 fighters on patrol encountered four British Martlets. In the ensuing dogfight, all three French and one British aircraft were shot down.

Captured French maps showed that the coastal batteries were well defended against a land attack. Such an attack, in Sturges' estimation, would take several days and cost around three hundred casualties. 17th Brigade moved up with artillery and tanks in support, ready to attack while 13th Brigade occupied the airport.

The SOE agents attached to Sturges' headquarters, after discussing the situation with Mayer and seeking his advice, offered to try to negotiate a surrender. At 09:50, a signal was sent to Syfret, asking for the naval bombardment to be delayed until 10:30. At 10:06, as negotiations were going well, he was asked to postpone it until further notice.

Syfret wasn't happy about this postponement. He later wrote in his report, "I was tired of this shilly-shallying and parleying for which I had given no authorisation, and which was keeping the Fleet steaming up and down in dangerous waters"[1]. He replied that he would commence a fifteen-minute bombardment to encourage the French to surrender. HMS *Ramillies*, *Hermione*, and *Lightning* opened fire at 10:40, then ceased fire ten minutes later, on hearing that the forces on the Orangea peninsula had surrendered.

The batteries had raised white flags soon after the barrage began. Lieutenant Colonel Hugh Stockwell, the commander of the 2nd Battalion Royal Welch Fusiliers, went forward with Julius Hanau (code-named "Caesar") of the SOE and a French military doctor to take the surrender. By 15:00 the forts of the Joffre Line, Fort Caimans and Fort Bellevue, had also surrendered. British minesweepers swept the channel leading to Diego Suarez Bay, and at 17:30 *Ramillies*, *Hermione*, *Lightning*, and *Paladin* entered the bay and laid anchor. The ships still anchored off Courrier Bay set off for Diego Suarez Bay at 16:00 on 7th May and at 05:00 on 8th May. They entered Diego Suarez Bay and laid anchor on the 8th.

The fight for the harbour at Diego Suarez was now over, but Syfret's ships weren't completely out of danger. The Vichy French submarine *Monge* was stationed off the entrance to Diego Suarez Bay. Just before 08:00 on 8th May, she fired torpedoes at the aircraft carrier *Indomitable*. The torpedo trails were spotted and *Indomitable* was able to evade them. The destroyer *Active* already had a sonar contact on *Monge*, and she was soon sunk by depth charges. *Indomitable* and her escorts continued into the anchorage. The carrier *Illustrious* remained outside the bay, along with her escorts, to provide anti-submarine and fighter cover. They entered the harbour on 9th May.

Admiral Syfret accepted the formal surrender of the French forces in Diego Suarez on board *Ramillies* at 17:30 on 8th May 1942. The next day, Churchill sent a message of congratulations to Admiral Syfret and General Sturges. In an extra note to 29th Independent Infantry Brigade, whom he had observed in training some months before, he wrote, "I was sure when I saw you at Inverary nine months ago that the 29th Brigade Group would make its mark."[2]

The harbour at Diego Suarez was now in British hands. Despite previous experience of hostility from Vichy French forces, the planners had hoped that they would encounter only token opposition, and had been proved wrong. Still, Operation Ironclad had succeeded, and provided some good news for the Allies at a time when it was in short supply.

British casualties were 109 killed or missing and 284 wounded. In addition, nine aircraft were lost and five damaged. Only one ship was lost, the minesweeper HMS *Auricula*. French casualties were slightly greater at 145 killed and 336 wounded, and seventeen aircraft had been destroyed. French naval losses included the sloop *D'Entrecasteaux*, the auxiliary cruiser *Bougainville*, and the submarines *Le Héros, Monge,* and *Bévéziers*.

The various branches of the armed forces and the SOE had worked well together. Admiral Syfret later said that "cooperation between the services was most cordial"[3]. Lieutenant Colonel John Todd, the head of SOE's East Africa Mission, reported that General Sturges had described Mayer's efforts as "the finest bit of Fifth Column work he had heard of."[4]

The Earl of Selborne had taken up the position of Minister for Economic Warfare, which included responsibility for SOE, in February 1942. The creation of SOE had been controversial, and it still had enemies. It was therefore useful for Selborne to have such a notable success so soon after taking over.

Operation Ironclad preceded more famous amphibious invasions such as those of Operations Torch and Overlord. As the first, it provided useful experience and lessons for those later operations. It was the first time that Britain had used tanks in an amphibious operation, and proved the utility of the tank landing ship concept. *Bachaquero*'s difficulties reaching the beach led to the addition of causeways on tank landing ships to bridge any gap from the ship to the beach. The advance on Diego Suarez was the only time that Tetrarchs were used in their originally intended role of standard light tanks. The next time they were used was in the Normandy invasion, where they were dropped in gliders to provide armoured support to the airborne forces.

From observations around the use of carrier-borne aircraft, the Mobile Operational Naval Air Base concept was born, which was used successfully in the Pacific theatre. The dummy paratroopers dropped on 5th May were also a resounding success, having drawn out an elite company on a wild goose chase. The idea was used again during the airborne landings that formed part of Operation Overlord, the invasion of Normandy.

Admiral Syfret's report included a number of lessons learned and recommendations for future operations. One notable inclusion was that white flags and leaflets should not be employed when operating against French possessions. He dryly noted that "Stories of what the inhabitants did with the leaflets would surprise their originators." Having also had the task of dealing with the news media, he suggested that future operations should have a Press Liaison Officer on the staff to handle journalists.

The War Office noted that surprise had been a major contributor to the success of the operation. They suggested that instead of securing beaches, leading formations might be better employed exploiting deep into enemy territory. This would spread the threat to the enemy, and might offer greater protection to later forces than any covering screen that they would be able to provide.[5]

Against the advice of the local SOE agents, the British decided not to occupy any more of the island, because the forces used for the invasion were needed elsewhere. SOE, particularly Mayer, argued that they should at least extend the occupation to a line from Antalaha in the east to Ambanja in the west. This was a small portion of the island, which SOE's intelligence suggested could be taken and held without any great difficulty. The area produced various useful products which would greatly ease the logistical challenge of feeding both the garrison and the local population.

The surrender treaty conference at Diego Suarez

SOE had agents in the unoccupied portion of the island, including Berthe Mayer, and they had come under increased suspicion following the invasion. Following Percy Mayer's arrest, the homes of Berthe Mayer, Richard Mayer (Percy's brother) and another agent were searched, and all three were put under close surveillance[6]. All British subjects were submitted to close scrutiny, and Richard Mayer in particular was ordered to close his house, located some miles outside Majunga, and move into the town to facilitate the authorities' surveillance of him. The French used radio direction finding equipment and carefully timed electricity blackouts to locate radio transmitters. Despite this, all the SOE agents continued to carry out their work, relaying information about the Vichy French forces and administration to the British in the north.

The Royal Army Ordnance Corps (RAOC) set up workshops in the naval arsenal at Diego Suarez and repaired the damaged tanks, as well as the coastal guns that had been hit during the operation. The British Admiralty wanted to use Diego Suarez as the main base for the

Eastern Fleet, but Admiral Somerville disagreed, citing the lack of security while most of the island was under Vichy control.

The Allied press was happy to print headlines celebrating the capture of Diego Suarez, but de Gaulle was angry that the operation had taken place without his knowledge. In fact, he first heard of the operation when a journalist rang him at 03:00 to get his reaction. Publicly, he claimed that the majority of the French on Madagascar supported his position, although the truth was that he had very little support on the island. Brigadier Lush, in charge of organising the civilian authorities, had advised London that there was no love for de Gaulle on the island, and that introducing Free French forces was likely to cause a breakdown in law and order.

Anthony Eden, the Foreign Secretary, met with de Gaulle on the 11th to try to smooth the latter's ruffled feathers. He assured de Gaulle that the participation of the Free French had received careful consideration, but ultimately they had not been invited to participate because "it was undesirable that Frenchmen should fight against Frenchmen". De Gaulle responded that he understood that such things might be necessary sometimes, and that "he might himself one day undertake an operation without consulting anybody."[7] One thing he had in common with the Vichy French authorities was a suspicion that the British wanted to expand their empire at French expense. The British would not allow Free French forces to land at Madagascar, but de Gaulle made plans for an invasion of the nearby island of Réunion. A Free French force, without British support, took that island in November 1942.

On 13th May 1942, the German naval chief of staff,

Admiral Fricke, met the Japanese attaché and urged him to recommend action against the British on Madagascar. Fricke argued that a counter-attack now, before the British had time to establish themselves, would have a good chance of success. The possibility was discussed several times in Germany and Japan until Allied successes in the Pacific persuaded the Japanese navy against any moves further west.

A South African fighter squadron equipped with Martin Marylands and Bristol Beauforts was moved to Arrachart airfield to provide air cover for the British forces. Two Fleet Air Arm squadrons, equipped with Fulmar fighters and Albacore torpedo bombers, joined them, as did six Westland Lysanders for army cooperation duties. Lockheed Lodestar and Junkers Ju-52 transport aircraft were used for logistical support.

On 20th May, the 13th Brigade embarked to leave for Bombay. This was made easier because most of their stores had not been unloaded, but many of them had contracted malaria and dengue fever. This was a problem that would continue to plague the British in Madagascar.

Also on the 20th, *Oronsay* sailed to Durban, carrying most of the prisoners of war captured during the campaign. This included 947 French and 402 Senegalese, as well as seventy Italians, fifty-five Germans, and seventy-five civilians who were related to the prisoners. Once they arrived in South Africa, the French and Senegalese were given the option of avoiding internment by joining de Gaulle's Free French. All of the Senegalese soldiers accepted the offer, but none of the French did so.

Three days later on the 23rd, four assault ships, escorted by two corvettes and two destroyers, sailed to Kilindini to collect the 22nd East African Brigade. The

East Africans were to take over from the 17th Brigade, so that the latter could be transferred to India. The 17th Brigade sailed on 12th June. Later in June, the South African 7th Motorised Brigade Group arrived in Madagascar, bringing with them twenty Marmon-Herrington armoured cars. These were mostly the Mark III version, armed with a Boys anti-tank rifle and Vickers machine gun in a turret. A few were the earlier Mark II, armed with twin Vickers machine guns[8]. Both versions were based on a lorry chassis and had four-wheel drive.

By the end of May, Force F had been broken up, and most of the ships had sailed to join the Eastern or Mediterranean Fleet. Only *Ramillies* and two Flower-class corvettes remained at Diego Suarez. Operational control of Madagascar had been transferred to East Africa Command, under Lieutenant-General Sir William Platt.

9

"LIVE AND LET LIVE"

With Diego Suarez taken, Smuts once again pressed for the occupation of the whole island. He was particularly concerned about the ports of Tamatave and Majunga. He pointed out that French submarines had used them, and Japanese submarines could easily do the same. Churchill, however, disagreed. In an April letter to General Ismay he said, "Getting this place is meant to be a help and not a new burden."[1] In a message to Admiral Syfret on 15th May he used very similar language, stating that "It [Madagascar] must be a security and not a burden."[2]

With this in mind, Syfret was instructed to make Diego Suarez secure with the smallest forces possible. If he considered it feasible to take Tamatave and Majunga in the next few days, he could do so, then send the 13th and 17th Brigade to India. Alternatively, he could work towards a peaceful co-existence with the Vichy-controlled part of the island. He could offer trade deals (most of the island was still blockaded by the Royal Navy) and threaten military action in order to secure cooperation. The admiral replied that he expected the French to adopt a policy of "live and let live"[3], which he would also adopt. Anything else would require a significant application of force in order to occupy Tamatave and Majunga.

The British didn't know it, but the French were determined to make them pay dearly for any further encroachment onto Vichy territory. A telegram from General Guillemet, Annet's senior military commander, illustrated this. "We are determined to make the most of our means and make the attacker pay dearly for any attack aimed at occupying the defended points."[4] On 9th May the Vichy Secretary of State for the Colonies had sent a stirring telegram to Annet. It drew parallels between the current invasion and Joan of Arc's fifteenth century campaigns against England. "Against the same invader, the French island shows the same courage. It is the most beautiful tribute that is paid to Joan of Arc: the sacrifice to the Fatherland and the confidence in her destiny."[5]

Back in France, the public were subjected to similar Anglophobic rhetoric over the following months, with old arguments being rehashed to portray the British as opportunists looking to enrich themselves at France's expense. Pamphlets were distributed within France itself and French colonies in North Africa, presumably considered likely to be subject to a similar attack. Posters were commissioned and displayed in both Paris and the non-occupied areas. The propaganda was generally blunt, and despite a heavy-handed control over the press, it was not always effective.

The British retaliated with their own propaganda. The BBC World Service broadcast the British justification for the invasion. The government commissioned Alfred

Hitchcock to make the anti-Vichy film *Aventure Malgache*, although this wasn't released until 1944.

On 27th May, a British businessman named Leslie Barnett arrived in Diego Suarez. Barnett worked for the Standard Vacuum Oil Company of South Africa and was also an SOE agent, operating under the symbol DZ/14. The businessmen of Madagascar were keen to resume trade with Britain, and Barnett had used this as an excuse to secure permission to travel between Vichy-held and British-held areas of the island. Governor Annet had asked him to talk to the British and try to secure a lifting of the blockade, and a recognition from the British of a neutral Vichy sovereignty over the rest of the island, in order to "save further bloodshed"[6]. Barnett delivered the message, along with intelligence that jamming had prevented him transmitting by radio, and added his own observation that Annet was playing for time.[7] If Annet could make the negotiations drag on until November, the rains would make it very difficult for the British to carry out any military action.

Barnett returned to Tananarive on the 28th with the British proposals for an agreement. They wanted to occupy the other key ports on the island, and for Annet to agree to continue negotiations on an official basis. In return, they would allow Annet to continue his governorship over the rest of the island. The next day, however, telegrams from London forbade any negotiations with Annet without reference to London.

The British government was divided over the question of Madagascar. Churchill was happy to leave Annet in place, but Foreign Secretary Eden strongly opposed the idea, and wanted a Free French governor in place as soon as possible. Eden's desire for a Free French governor heading a civilian administration led to a dispute with the War Office, who considered Diego Suarez to be occupied enemy territory, and therefore under military jurisdiction. Eventually, they reached a compromise where a Foreign Office official shared responsibility for political and economic administration with Brigadier Lush.

The Foreign Office wanted Free French governorship over Madagascar so that it would become an active ally in the war effort and not be merely neutral. One reason for this was the presence of raw materials that were needed for munitions. Mica, rock crystal, and rubber were all found on Madagascar, and were in short supply for the Allies. High-quality graphite, required for the development of atomic weapons, was also present on the island.

Annet relayed the British proposals to Marshal Pétain, and was ordered to reject them. Barnett returned to Diego Suarez on 5th June 1942, but there was no sign that Annet would accept the proposals.

Meanwhile, at about 22:30 on 29th May, an aircraft flew over the harbour at Diego Suarez. It was a Yokosuka E14Y ("Glen" to the Allies) from the Japanese submarine *I-10*, but it was not positively identified. Extra vigilance was ordered, and preparations were made for an expected dawn attack from the air or sea. *Ramillies* was under steam well before dawn and moved anchor to a new location at 05:00 on 30th May. Air patrols were mounted at dawn and throughout the day, and the corvettes still based at Diego Suarez increased their patrols, but they found nothing.

Then at 20:25, an enormous explosion announced a torpedo hit on *Ramillies*. Two Japanese midget submarines, launched from the parent submarines *I-16* and *I-20*, had entered the harbour, and one had managed to hole the battleship in the bow. *Ramillies* settled at the bow but remained afloat. By discharging ammunition and oil, she was able to regain her trim well enough to sail for Durban the following day, reaching there on 9th June. She was out of action for several months.

Around 21:00, a second explosion was heard. The tanker SS *British Loyalty* had just got under way when her master saw torpedo tracks heading towards *Ramillies*. Living up to his ship's name, he altered course so that they would hit his ship instead. The tanker quickly sank.

This was what Churchill had always feared, albeit on a much smaller scale: Japanese naval forces based in the western Indian Ocean, ready to prey on convoys bound for India and the Far East. Not that the local authorities realised this at the time. They assumed that Vichy French forces had mounted the attacks, and they mounted retaliatory raids against airfields in the south.

On 1st June, locals informed the commandoes still stationed in Cap Diego that two foreigners had been sighted about twenty kilometres to the south. A patrol of two officers and thirteen men was dispatched. The local population was very helpful, volunteering information on the last known whereabouts of the Japanese sailors. The marines reached the village of Ano Vondrona around midnight. The chief of the village refused to help at night, saying that the British made too much noise, but offered help the next morning. At 04:00 the patrol set off, with sixteen locals from the village. The locals found footprints, and the Japanese sailors were found at around 07:00 on 2nd June.

When called upon to surrender, one sailor gave a Nazi salute, and the other drew and fired a revolver, before both ran for cover. They were killed and buried where they were found. A note found on one of them was taken back and translated, which indicated that they were from a submarine of the 1st Division of the 8th Submarine Flotilla. The chief of the village that had originally reported the presence of the Japanese sailors was brought back to Diego Suarez so that Major-General Sturges could thank him in person.

Field Marshal Smuts wasted no time in using the torpedo attack to argue once again for the occupation of the whole of Madagascar, sending a message to Churchill on 1st June. He suggested that the attack "must have been made by Vichy submarine or by Japanese submarine on Vichy information and advice."[8] He offered a South African brigade group to help conquer the rest of the island.

The admiralty, though, believed that the midget submarine had been brought by a larger submarine which also carried a reconnaissance aircraft. They believed the midget submarine crew had scuttled their craft, then got ashore. Churchill noted that if this was correct, the Vichy French might not be involved[9]. An interpreter was flown to Madagascar to read the crew's notes.

The Vichy French had not aided the Japanese, but only because they had not been asked for help. When Annet asked for guidance should a Japanese submarine ask for assistance, he was told that a request "to stay in a Madagascar port longer than normal under international law" should be granted. The 8th Submarine Flotilla did not make any such requests, using supply ships instead. After the harbour attack, they conducted operations against merchant ships in the Mozambique Channel. During June and July, they sank a total of twenty-five merchantmen, totalling over 120,000 tons.

Smuts continued to argue for occupation of the entire island, and his views were shared by Lord Harlech, the High Commissioner to South Africa. In a telegram on 6th June, he referred to the "extreme danger of hesitation further over policy of getting complete and effective control of whole island."[10]

On 21st June the president of the Planters' Association, Monsieur Millot, arrived in Diego Suarez. He had received permission from Annet to travel for business, but was also carrying out an unofficial mission for Captain Fauché, Annet's aide-de-camp.

Millot informed the British that, with a few exceptions, the civilians and military on the island wanted an agreement with the British. Annet was too timid to take the initiative, but his request for instructions from Vichy had gone unanswered. He suggested that the British propose negotiations aimed at finding a way for the British and Vichy to live together, but without any explicit threat of force, since that would force Vichy to order resistance. Alternatively, an overwhelming force would allow Annet to surrender with honour, and his superiors in Vichy would see that he had no choice.

Around the same time, plans were being drawn up to take the rest of the island. The British hoped that the planned attacks would be enough to persuade Annet to surrender with little resistance. This was not to be.

As Madagascar was now being considered part of East Africa Command, it was decided that the island of Mayotte, off the west coast, had to be taken. It had a powerful radio station, the neighbouring island of Pamanzi had an airfield, and it was ideally placed to intercept shipping travelling between Madagascar and East Africa. Although its defences comprised fewer than one hundred armed police, intelligence suggested that key installations had been rigged with explosives so that they could be destroyed if a landing was attempted. The commander and his men were known to be loyal to Vichy, and the British had finally learned that Vichy forces would regard them as enemies, so they expected resistance, although the civilian population was thought to be friendly. A staff officer who had visited the island in 1938 provided intelligence on buildings and tracks.[11] Care was taken to ensure that the planned operation remained a tightly kept secret.

The planned operation was given the codename Operation Throat. The invading force comprised one cruiser, HMS *Dauntless*, a destroyer, HMS *Active*, thirty men from 4 Troop of 5 Commando, and C Company of the 5th Battalion, King's African Rifles. There were signals, intelligence, and mortar detachments in support. The small force set off on 30th June 1942. In order to maximise surprise and minimise resistance, the landing was planned to take place before dawn on 2nd July.

The King's African Rifles landed quietly at the main port of Mamoudzou. Surprise was almost absolute, with the Chef de District and many police being caught in bed. The chief of police and a few others tried to escape by car, but were stopped at roadblocks.

The first commando detachment landed on Dzaoudzi at 02:33 and found steps carved in the rock which led to a path to the radio station. They were under strict instructions not to fire unless fired upon, and wore strips of white cloth around their necks to aid recognition. At 02:40 the commandoes captured the radio station intact. The radio operator was captured fully dressed and about to enter the station, having been alerted by locals who had heard the landing craft engines.

At 02:50 the rest of the commandoes landed on the White Beach jetty, further to the west. One platoon moved to the hospital while the rest of the detachment headed to Government House, where they captured the Governor of the Comoros group of islands, which included Mayotte. That afternoon, the rest of the island of Pamanzi was taken, including its airfield.

Operation Throat had been a complete success. The islands of Mayotte and Pamanzi were occupied with no loss of life and with all facilities intact. The islands became bases for RAF Catalina flying boats, which flew regular anti-submarine patrols.

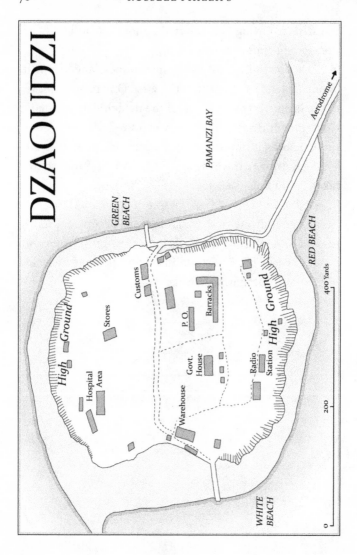

<h1 align="center">10</h1>

<h1 align="center">OPERATION STREAMLINE JANE</h1>

A s SOE agents had warned, the British struggled to provide sufficient provisions to the occupying forces and the local population. As a partial solution, they extended the area under their control in order to gain greater access to resources.

Field Marshall Smuts held a conference in Pretoria on 20th June, with Generals Platt and Sturges, Admiral Willis, and Lord Harlech. They concluded that negotiations should continue, with the aim of leaving the existing authorities in place but subject to British control, including censorship and control of external communications. If the Vichy French would not agree to these terms, Majunga would be captured and occupied. The offer would then be made again, and if refused, forces would push on to threaten Tananarive. If the French still refused the terms, Tananarive would be taken and occupied.[1]

The entire campaign would have to be concluded before the rains began in the autumn. Poor internal communications links on the island meant that amphibious landings would be required. This meant that

29th Independent Infantry Brigade's move to India had to
be postponed, so that its specialised training could be put
to use. Assault shipping, which had already been sent on
to India, would have to be returned.

This proposal was put to London, with a request for a
quick decision. Admiral Somerville backed the plan,
saying that occupation of the whole of Madagascar would
allow him to free up ships to operate in Burma and
Malaya. At the end of June, the Chiefs of Staff refused the
plan, citing reverses in the Middle East and the possibility
of a Japanese invasion of India. Instead, the British on the
island were to redouble their efforts to negotiate a deal
with the Vichy administration under Annet.

By the middle of July, it had become obvious that
Annet was simply playing for time, hoping to keep negotiations going until the autumn rains made military action
impossible. Platt again asked London for permission to
occupy the remainder of the island and made it clear he
needed a quick decision in order to finish the campaign
before the autumn. The situation in India was now much
less dire, and on 19th July 1942, Churchill told the Chiefs
of Staff to "tidy up" in Madagascar.[2] As with Operation
Ironclad, the Free French were not to be involved, and de
Gaulle would be left in the dark until the start date.

The Chiefs of Staff were concerned that there was not
enough assault shipping to go around and that it would
have a negative impact on Operation Torch in North
Africa, and so they recommended suspending operations
in Madagascar.[3] Anthony Eden supported the operation,
noting that the United States had an interest in obtaining
supplies of mica and graphite from the island.[4] He further
noted that terms of surrender should not promise uncon-
ditional repatriation of Vichy forces, since the British

could use them as leverage to secure the release of British troops held in Vichy France. Ultimately, the Chiefs of Staff were overruled.

Intelligence suggested that Vichy forces were not large. Estimates suggested that Annet had a little over six thousand infantry, fifteen artillery pieces, seven aircraft, a sloop and a submarine. They had an ample supply of machine guns and 81mm mortars, but were short of ammunition for rifles and machine guns. In addition, there were an unknown number of armed police. Enemy numbers weren't a significant problem therefore, but the terrain was another story. The few roads through the dense forest were of poor quality, making any advance difficult, and the close terrain favoured defence rather than attack.

Three primary operations were planned, codenamed Stream, Line, and Jane. These three operations were sometimes written together as Operation Streamline Jane or Stream-Line-Jane. Two diversionary and supporting operations were planned, named Operations Esme and Tamper.

Operation Stream was to be an amphibious assault on Majunga by the 29th Independent Infantry Brigade. Once the port was secure, Operation Line would begin, with the 22nd East African Brigade landing and advancing on Tananarive, the island's capital. Operation Jane involved the 29th again, this time sailing around to the port of Tamatave on the east of the island. They would then advance on the capital, where they would meet up with the East Africans.

Operation Esme would see the South African Brigade advance south from Sakaramy, eight kilometres north-east of Joffreville, to draw forces away from the centre of the island, and a small force would take the island of Nossi-bé. In Operation Tamper, elements of 5 Commando would land at Morondava, in an effort to draw forces away from the main attack. To support the South African advance south as part of Esme, SOE were asked to provide intelligence on the road between Ambilobe and Majunga. Berthe Mayer sent a detailed radio report from Tananarive, giving the locations of roadblocks, bridges, guns, and enemy forces.

Maryland photo-reconnaissance aircraft of the South African Air Force flew missions over Tananarive and the ports of Majunga and Tamatave, where the amphibious landings were planned to take place. One aircraft, commanded by an officer named Jones, was hit by anti-aircraft fire and made a forced landing on the east coast. The pilot used the aeroplane's radio to contact his base, and a rescue party was dispatched. They failed to get through, but air drops kept the three crewmen supplied. The French sent a force of native troops commanded by a French officer to capture the airmen, but local Malagasy warned Jones, and he decided to ambush them. The crew removed a Vickers K machine gun from the aircraft and set it up to cover Jones, who stood in the open, waiting for the French. When the French arrived, a burst from the machine gun was sufficient to persuade them to surrender. The crew and their forty prisoners continued to be supplied by air until a ship arrived from Diego Suarez to pick them up.

29th Independent Infantry Brigade took part in a large amphibious landing exercise in Kenya named Exercise Touchstone, where they assaulted Mombasa. Secrecy concerns meant that the troops were told that it was to test Mombasa's defences, but of course it was really a rehearsal for their part in Operation Stream. Reinforcements arrived from the UK while the brigade was in Mombasa, and rumours began to circulate about what was in store next. A single South African regiment was given some training in amphibious landings.

Later in July, word arrived that the manager of the Banque de Madagascar, a Monsieur Dupont, was en route to Diego Suarez as a representative of Annet. It appeared once more that it might be possible to reach a negotiated settlement. Dupont was not allowed into Diego Suarez and was instead met by Laurence Grafftey-Smith from the Foreign Office at Ambilobe. Dupont's instructions were to continue the talks that had started in May with Barnett. Annet still refused to enter official discussions, so they made little progress.

Grafftey-Smith did persuade Dupont to part with millions of francs to ease the financial strain in Diego Suarez. Dupont was reluctant, but agreed when it was pointed out that the alternative was to introduce sterling. The British had an ample supply of British Military Administration sterling notes, but were wary of issuing them, fearing that doing so would provide ammunition to Vichy's claims that the invasion was intended to enlarge the British empire at the cost of the French.

In August, the Japanese submarine *I-29* arrived north of Madagascar. During August and September, it sank four Allied merchant ships. The British took this as evidence that Annet was giving assistance to the Japanese. This wasn't true, but they didn't know that, and it helped to justify their plan to occupy the whole island.

The island of Nossi-bé, defended by thirty-five men with four machine guns, was to be taken by a force designated NOSCOL, made up of a detachment of Royal

Marines and two platoons of Pretoria Highlanders from South Africa. The marines travelled on the minelayer *Manxman*, while the Highlanders were on rowing boats towed behind. At 02:00 on 9th September, the Royal Marines landed at Hell-Ville on the south of the island. They captured a sugar mill, but then came under machine gun fire in a swamp and had to retreat, having suffered three wounded.

The Pretoria Highlanders conducted the first assault landing by South African infantry, landing at 02:45, under cover of a bombardment from *Manxman* and fire from their own machine guns. By 08:00 the island had been taken and the Vichy French commander had surrendered. The South Africans remained on the island as a garrison force.

11

OPERATION STREAM

At 15:00 on 5th September, a convoy left Mombasa with the 29th Independent Infantry Brigade and the South African Armoured Car Commando aboard, to begin Operation Stream. Another convoy left Diego Suarez on 7th September. The entire force of almost seventy ships, known as Force M, rendezvoused about one hundred and fifty kilometres south of Mayotte on 9th September.

The plan was for the Royal Welch Fusiliers and East Lancashires to land around fifteen kilometres to the north of Majunga on a beach designated Red Beach, at 22:00 on 9th September. They would then attack the port from landward. The supporting tank squadron was also to land at Red Beach, but in the event, Majunga was taken so quickly that they remained on board ship.[1]

At 02:10, the South Lancashires and 5 Commando would land to the west of the town, on Green Beach. One company of the Royal Scots Fusiliers would land on Brown Beach to attack suspected gun positions on the

Datsepe Peninsula, with the rest remaining as a floating reserve.

After some delays, the first wave landed on Red Beach at around 01:00 on 10th September. They started making their way towards the town, using three roads which were little more than tracks. Some units had difficulty finding their assigned roads, and so progress was slow. There were some skirmishes, but no serious resistance until they reached the edge of the town. The second wave, made up of two companies of the Royal Welch Fusiliers, moved around to the south-east, then turned north to advance into Majunga itself.

The military commander in Majunga, Chef de Bataillon Martins, was alerted to the British attack from the north. He reacted exactly as the British planners had hoped, and ordered troops out of Majunga to the north. This left Majunga itself with little to oppose the impending attack from the South Lancashires and 5 Commando.

The first assault troops landed on Green Beach at 05:18, and were met by fire from two machine guns. They formed up quickly and returned fire at short range, silencing the guns. They quickly cleared the docks and moved into the town. Unlike Operation Ironclad, there was no warning given, and the French forces were taken so completely by surprise that the British took eighty prisoners in the first eight minutes.

At dawn, aircraft from HMS *Illustrious* and South African Air Force (SAAF) aircraft from Mayotte flew overhead, providing support. The British ground troops used red umbrellas as a recognition signal.[2] Royal Navy personnel tasked with preventing sabotage in the port were hindered by snipers at first, until men of 5 Commando were able to deal with them. A single troop from 5 Commando paddled boats up the River Ikopa, using grenades to ward off crocodiles. They were to cut off any Vichy forces retreating from Majunga, but in the event the French made no attempt to retreat.

The airfield was in Allied hands by 06:05, the barracks and post office by 06:33. Chef de Bataillon Martins was captured and ordered to surrender, but he refused to do so until the British assured him that his men had fought valiantly. That done, British and French officers drove around the town ordering the troops to cease fire. It was all over by 07:00. Reports of British casualties vary, but they were very low, with no more than a dozen killed.

British warships entered the harbour after it had been swept for mines. Vichy sympathisers were identified and rounded up. 29th Independent Infantry Brigade was re-embarked onto ships in preparation for Operation Jane.

Operation Tamper was a diversion mounted in support of Operation Stream. A single troop from 5 Commando landed at Morondava harbour, about 560km south of Majunga. They were transported on the destroyer HMAS *Napier* and landed in daylight to no opposition.

A road ran from Morondava to Tananarive, so it was a potential landing point for a force intending to advance on the capital. The men of 5 Commando arrested the Vichy Chef de District and replaced the French Tricolour with a Union Jack. A party was dispatched inland to secure billets for a much larger force that they carelessly "revealed" was due to arrive soon.

To add to the deception and hopefully draw troops

away from the actual fighting, a British-Moroccan sergeant who spoke fluent French made a telephone call to Tananarive. Claiming to be the Chef de District, he said that a large force had landed, and that it was futile to resist. The secretary who took the call suspected it was a hoax, but it appears that a small force was sent from Majunga just in case.

Having done what they could to distract the Vichy forces from Operation Stream, they re-embarked on *Napier* to re-join their comrades at Majunga.

A South African force was formed to drive south from Diego Suarez. Designated GETCOL, it consisted of a battalion from the First City Regiment, a battery of 25-pounders, a field engineer company, a field ambulance unit, and eight armoured cars. GETCOL left their start point of Sakaramy at 20:00 on 9th September and made quick progress as far as Beramanja. From there progress was slow, hampered by roadblocks formed from cut-down trees.

A South African armoured car and crew on Madagascar

Terrain and mosquitoes were major problems. There were hundreds of rivers and ravines to cross, and the Vichy forces had destroyed all bridges capable of carrying heavy vehicles. All the men were bitten by mosquitoes, which were an ever-present problem.

The first strong Vichy position was at Ambazoana, just behind the Ambazoana River, a tidal river with a sixty-metre-long bridge. The defensive position overlooked about two hundred metres of road flanked by swamps. It was a strong position if attacked from the north, but it was open to attack from the south. A party was landed on the coast behind the Vichy lines and attacked the position from the rear, to little opposition.

A single detached company from First City Regiment, with attached signallers and medics, was designated SEACOL. This force was transported in six dhows and landed near Antanambo with the intention of cutting off Vichy communications and line of retreat. They were too late, however, and reunited with GETCOL on 11th September. On the 12th, GETCOL's commander, Lieutenant Colonel Getcliffe, contacted the Royal Navy and arranged for the forces on Nossi-bé to be landed south of Maromandia. His intention was that the retreating Vichy forces would be caught between the two Allied forces.

The Vichy forces, however, made a stand. A motor-cycle reconnaissance platoon was operating ahead of the main GETCOL force, and on the evening of 13th September, they encountered strong resistance twelve kilometres south of the Djangoa River at Jojahely. The infantry arrived late the next day and patrols were sent out on the night of 14th September. These were met with machine gun and rifle fire, indicating that the defenders intended to put up a stiff resistance. When the political officer attached to GETCOL demanded surrender, the Vichy commander told him that their orders were to fight to the last man. An engineer officer set off to make a lone reconnaissance, and ten minutes later a loud explosion was heard. He was never seen again, and it was assumed that he had set off a mine or booby trap.

The 25-pounder battery arrived at around 11:00 on the 15th, and laid down a barrage on the defenders while the armoured cars drove up to the first roadblocks. A few felled trees were cleared, but machine gun fire made it impossible to do more. Getcliffe reluctantly decided that an infantry attack was necessary and gave orders for the infantry to prepare.

Just as the African infantry were about to begin their assault at 13:15, the Vichy forces raised a white flag. Getcliffe refused to discuss terms unless all forces as far as Maromandia were included in the arrangement. The French agreed and called the forces at Ankaramy, who agreed to surrender. The forces from Nossi-bé landed on 15th September and marched forty kilometres to Maro-mandia. They arrived on 16th September, to discover that the Vichy forces had already surrendered.

With no active enemy forces ahead of them, GETCOL entered their objective of Maromandia on 18th September. A patrol was sent south to meet with a contingent from Majunga, and they met on 22nd September. The Diego Suarez-Majunga road was now clear and in Allied hands.

A small force designated VOLCOL left Beramanja on 9th September, heading down the east coast to Antalaha. It consisted of a platoon of infantry and six armoured cars, supported by a mortar detachment, engineers, and medics. The small force had to cross five major rivers to reach the coast at Vohemar, which they entered on 11th September. They had faced no opposition, but the local Chef de Région refused to accept their authority, and was arrested.

VOLCOL resumed its advance southwards on the 16th,

once again having to cross several major and many smaller rivers. The engineers were often called upon to repair damaged bridges or deploy their single girder bridge to allow the column to continue. The final river was crossed using locally sourced pontoons, and VOLCOL entered the town of Antalaha on 24th September 1942.

12

OPERATION LINE

The 22nd East African Brigade had the task of advancing from Majunga to Tananarive, a distance of around 570km. The brigade was split into three fighting groups (designated Number 1, Number 2, and Number 3), and a forward body. Each fighting group had a battalion of infantry, a battery of artillery, and a troop of three armoured cars. The forward body had a company of infantry, with supporting mortars, engineers, and armoured cars.

The road to Tananarive crossed two main bridges over the Kamaro and Betsiboka rivers. General Platt asked for paratroopers to seize the bridges, but the Chiefs of Staff said that none were available, and so SOE were assigned the task of securing them[1]. SOE planned to ensure the bridges remained intact in two ways: First, they would cut telephone wires so that no orders could be sent from Majunga or Tananarive to the local commanders at the bridge. Second, two parties would be put ashore to capture the bridges. In the event, neither plan worked.

For an unknown reason, the SOE agents were told to

cut the telephone wires on 11th September[2]. Consequently, the lines were still intact when the landing took place on the 10th. *Frontier*, the SOE boat that would land the parties, was spotted by a French patrol vessel. She managed to get away, but was only able to land one of the two parties. Although the French had not captured *Frontier*, their suspicions were roused, and they captured the party that had been landed.

Majunga did not have a quayside deep enough for the transport ships, so it would take days for the 22nd East African Brigade to finish disembarking. Knowing this, the forward body went ahead in an attempt to take the bridges before they could be destroyed by the French. The forward body had a troop of armoured cars, a company of infantry with mortars, a light AA battery, and a detachment of engineers. They hoped to capture both bridges by the evening.[3]

Leaving Majunga at 11:30 on 10th September, they reached the Kamaro bridge at 16:00, finding it intact and not prepared for demolition. The small Malagasy guard force was quickly driven off, and the bridge secured. The French were now in no doubt as to the invaders' intentions, and the Betsiboka River was still fifty kilometres further away. This river was crossed by a bridge with a total length of five hundred metres.

An SAAF squadron flew into Majunga North airfield early in the afternoon of 11th September. The SAAF could now mount patrols over the whole island, so the aircraft carrier *Illustrious* was able to leave Madagascar to join the Eastern Fleet.

The forward body set off at dawn on the 11th. Vichy forces had set roadblocks using felled trees. Despite these obstacles, the armoured cars reached the river at 06:30, to find that the largest bridge over the Betsiboka appeared to be destroyed. It was a suspension bridge, and the cables holding the central span (138m long) had been cut, leaving the span lying on the river bed.

First appearances were deceptive, though. The span was intact, and the water it lay in was just one metre deep. The Africans soon realised that they could still cross the bridge, although some care was needed since there was a steep descent and ascent at either end, in addition to wading through the river itself. Realising that the bridge was still usable, the French dispatched a Potez 63 bomber, but none of its bombs hit the bridge.

A small force had been left to defend the bridge, and when the Africans spotted movement on the far side, they hit the suspected positions with a mortar barrage. This, plus fire from the armoured cars, provided cover for two infantry platoons to cross the bridge. These platoons climbed the steep hillside and overcame the defenders, who had originally numbered eighty plus one hundred in reserve — many of those in reserve had run when the shooting began. Ten of the defenders were killed and forty taken prisoner, with the forward body suffering six wounded.

As soon as the defenders were defeated, engineers started work on the bridge. By nightfall on 12th September all the forward body had crossed the Betsiboka and the rest of Number 1 Fighting Group were close behind. A small force was left at the bridge, and the rest continued the advance.

The Vichy forces withdrew, making efforts to delay the advance as they went. Roads were blocked, telegraph wires cut, and transportation, oxen, and rice were removed. Annet told Vichy that, "Every day that passes allows us to ameliorate our defences on all our axis (sic) of penetration."

Resistance was encountered at Maevatanana, where the defenders blew up a petrol depot, and the vanguard reached Andriba on 14th September. The advance was resumed on the 16th, and a destroyed bridge was encountered over the River Mamokamita. A platoon of the King's African Rifles crossed the river on foot to reconnoitre. The defenders were well hidden, and held their fire until the platoon was within fifty metres. A mortar barrage was called down upon the defenders, and a second platoon crossed the river, under orders to cut the road behind the enemy's position.

The second platoon's commander was killed, but a sergeant named Odilo took over. He led a section to the rear of a machine gun position and destroyed it, before reorganising the platoon. He led the platoon in melee combat from the rear of the Vichy position, while the first platoon attacked from the front. Odilo was recommended for the Distinguished Conduct Medal, but was ultimately awarded the Military Medal (MM). Vichy casualties numbered fifty-two, including four French and eighteen Senegalese killed. The King's African Rifles lost five men killed and seven wounded.

The rest of Number 1 Fighting Group did not get over the river until the following night. The forward body continued on to Marotsipoy to secure the small landing strip there. Allied aircraft began using the landing strip on the afternoon of 18th September.

The advance continued, with good progress being made through the plains, the only sign of resistance being grass fires that had presumably been started by the retreating French. The force continued over a steep mountain, then came upon a defensive position at the Manankazo River. Opposition was light and soon overcome, although the subsequent advance was slowed by multiple roadblocks and destroyed bridges. The advance continued, though, and Ankazobe, less than a hundred kilometres from Tananarive, was reached by 20th September, ten days after the landing at Majunga.

Tananarive's primary defences were outside Mahitsy, twenty-five kilometres from the capital. The defensive line was three kilometres wide and, like the Joffre Line outside Diego Suarez, the positions were well camouflaged, making aerial reconnaissance difficult. The position was defended by three companies of infantry, supported by mortars, machine guns, and six artillery pieces (two 80mm, one 75mm, two 65mm, and a 37mm gun taken from an immobilised tank).

The SAAF flew a reconnaissance mission over the railway south of Tananarive, to check for trains taking supplies south. Trains were spotted, and so several attempts were made to bomb a railway bridge or the track to prevent the shipments. All the bombing attempts missed their targets.

At around 12:30 on 21st the forward body encountered the first line of defence. The road they were following crossed a valley on a causeway. French positions sited on the hills above overlooked the causeway. As they approached, the French opened fire with artillery, mortars, machine guns, and small arms. D Company of 1/1 King's African Rifles moved forward supported by armoured cars, but the infantry were pinned down by the French fire and the armoured cars had to take cover in a cutting.

By late afternoon, the locations of the French guns

had been determined, and as darkness approached three infantry companies attacked to the left, centre, and right of the French. A Company on the French left flank drove the enemy back about three hundred metres along the ridge before the French stood their ground and then mounted a counter-attack, covered by smoke from burning grass. A Company fell back, then rallied and resumed the attack, to find that the French had withdrawn.

On the French right flank, a small village and machine gun post were taken; then the company commander, Major Dawson, directed 25-pounder fire onto a French 75mm gun, which was soon destroyed.

At first light on 22nd September, A Company resumed their advance and captured an 80mm gun. Shortly after noon, RAF Lysanders were called in to bomb and strafe the French positions, and the defenders surrendered soon after.

RAF Westland Lysanders in flight over Madagascar

The armoured cars led the way once again, and it was soon discovered that the causeway had been broken in three places, each one covered by an enemy machine gun post. Two infantry companies were sent to flank the French positions while the rest of the fighting group removed obstructions to allow the armoured cars to advance. French artillery opened fire, wounding eleven men before being put out of action by the Allied armoured cars and artillery.

With the French artillery silenced, an infantry company went forwards and, after a two-hour fight, took the machine gun posts that were covering the causeway. The company then took the remainder of the Vichy defences at Mahitsy, in conjunction with the two flanking companies. The road to Tananarive was open.

The Allies expected heavy resistance on the final advance to Tananarive. Machine gun posts were known to be sited in pre-colonial forts on ridges, with added entrenchments. Annet, however, didn't plan to use them. The only remaining defence for Tananarive was a small force near Ivato airfield intended to delay the Allied advance while Annet and his remaining forces withdrew from the capital.

The Allies resumed the advance to Tananarive at dawn on 23rd September, with the forward body taking the lead. Light Vichy resistance was encountered eighteen kilometres from the capital, but mortar and machine gun fire dispersed the defenders without any great difficulty. As the force approached Ivato airfield, a second infantry company was sent ahead to support the forward body.

Defensive positions could be seen on a ridge overlooking the airfield, and both infantry companies went on the offensive. During the attack, Sergeant Walasi led his platoon in an attack on two field guns, capturing them before they could fire a single shot. He then attacked more defensive positions, taking a total of twenty prisoners. For these actions he was recommended for the Distinguished Conduct Medal, but this was reduced and he was awarded the Military Medal.

Tananarive was now completely undefended and Annet's secretary general, Ponvienne, declared it an open city. Operation Line had cost the Allies one officer and seven men dead, one officer and thirty-one men wounded.

General Platt set up his headquarters in Tananarive. He issued a proclamation announcing military jurisdiction with British maintenance of law and order, and set up an interim British administration. Ponvienne was interned because he refused to cooperate. Most of the French were still suspicious of Britain's motives in taking the island, and Britain's failure to clearly state its intentions for the future administration of the island did nothing to quell these suspicions.

Back in Britain, the public were generally pleased that their forces had taken the capital with few losses, but most had assumed that little resistance would be offered. Some were perplexed that the French had offered any resistance at all, showing a marked lack of understanding of the Vichy French position[4]. Field Marshal Smuts sent a telegram of congratulations to Platt, but the island still wasn't completely in Allied hands.

Annet had retreated south to Fianarantsoa, about three hundred kilometres south of Tananarive and the only large town not occupied by the Allies. From there, he sent a signal to the Colonial Ministry in Vichy, promising to "resist every enemy advance"[5]. He made radio broadcasts encouraging anti-British feeling, and even made direct telephone calls to officials in Tananarive, encouraging them not to cooperate with the British administration.

13

OPERATION JANE

2 9th Independent Infantry Brigade left Majunga on 13th September 1942 to sail to Tamatave for Operation Jane. The convoy included the battleship *Warspite*; the aircraft carrier *Illustrious*; three cruisers; and destroyers and minesweepers. Given the light opposition at Majunga, it was decided to try and intimidate the Tamatave garrison with a show of force.

The ships sailed into Tamatave harbour at daybreak on 18th September, and sent a radio signal to the defenders. The French refused to negotiate without permission from Tananarive. The British replied that representatives were being sent ashore on a boat under a white flag to discuss the British takeover of the town, and if the boat came under fire, the warships would bombard the town. Ten Swordfish from *Illustrious*, seven armed with bombs and three carrying dummy paratroopers, were ready to support the attack if necessary.

When the boat got to within about four hundred metres of the shore it was fired upon and turned back.

Once it had returned, the ships opened fire on their pre-designated targets. After just three minutes, Tamatave surrendered at 07:55.

29th Independent Infantry Brigade disembarked, some using landing craft, some directly onto the mole. The tanks of B and C Special Service Squadrons were landed from SS *Ocean Viking* on the 19th and 20th using makeshift flats. They were not used in the subsequent advance however, as the Ivondro River was found to be unfordable and the railway bridges were not suitable.[1]

The Vichy forces had left just eighty men at Tamatave. The others, including the artillery and machine guns, had withdrawn to Brickaville, eighty-five kilometres to the south. The brigade began the advance to the capital and soon discovered that the French had felled trees to create roadblocks. Eight of these were encountered in the first seven kilometres of the advance.

The British had a stroke of luck, however, as a goods train arrived in Tamatave station just before noon on the 18th. The 2nd Battalion South Lancashire Regiment boarded the train with a section of sappers. The British placed a railway official in a truck in front of the engine, hoping that he would know of the location of any mines. The train set off at 15:00. Progress was slow, with each bridge having to be carefully examined and precautions taken against ambushes.

The train had to stop after about ninety-five kilometres, still three kilometres short of Brickaville. Two bridges over a river had been destroyed, and so it could go no further. The South Lancashires headed towards Brickaville on foot, bypassing the river with the destroyed railway bridges. The larger Rianila River still had to be crossed, though. C Company investigated the possibility of crossing by ferry or wading, while B Company investigated the large road and railway bridge.

C Company found a boat, but B Company had discovered that the bridge was intact, so the battalion used the bridge. One platoon of B Company crossed in their stocking feet, sneaking up on forty Malagasy with a French officer. The rest of the battalion followed and cleared the town, securing it by 01:15 on 19th September. They suffered no casualties and took three French officers and eighty Malagasy prisoner.

Later on the 19th, A Company went ahead on the road to Tananarive, while the rest of the South Lancashires cleared multiple roadblocks in the area around Brickaville. The 1st Battalion Royal Scots Fusiliers arrived at Brickaville on the same day to support the South Lancashires, and on the 20th they sent a company forward to relieve the South Lancashire's A Company.

Meanwhile, 2nd Battalion Royal Welch Fusiliers were advancing on Tananarive. Their lead detachment of a company and a mortar detachment had requisitioned a variety of vehicles and animals to enable them to move more quickly, but they came to a halt when they reached the first destroyed bridge. This was repaired in under five hours, but they came upon another destroyed bridge a few kilometres later. Roadblocks and destroyed bridges were causing severe delays, so Lieutenant-Colonel Stockwell took a risk and split the battalion and the Royal Engineers up, to deal with several obstacles at a time. This left them vulnerable to enemy action, but no enemy opposition was encountered, and so the risk paid off.

The units advancing from Tamatave were still about

one hundred and fifty kilometres away from Tananarive when they heard of the capital's surrender on 23rd September.

14

OPERATION ROSE

T he capital had surrendered, but Annet was still at large, now based at Fianarantsoa and evidently intent on being a thorn in the Allied side. Annet's evasive tactics had already dragged the campaign on long enough to cause problems in the Far East, where an amphibious assault had to be cancelled because the landing craft were being used in September's operations on Madagascar. The rainy season was fast approaching, and the Allies needed to capture the rest of the island before it started.

General Platt and Admiral Tennant held a conference in Diego Suarez, where Platt brought up the possibility of a landing on the east coast. Tennant advised against it because of unsuitable beaches, and suggested occupying Tuléar on the west coast instead, even though this would require a longer advance on land.

A force comprising three companies of the Pretoria Regiment, a troop of armoured cars, and engineer support was formed under Lieutenant Colonel Engelbrecht. They embarked on the troopship SS *Empire Pride* and sailed with a small naval force headed by the cruiser HMS *Birmingham*. Admiral Tennant placed two hundred Royal Marines under Engelbrecht's command for Operation Rose — the occupation of Tuléar.

The small naval force entered Tuléar harbour at 06:30 on 29th September, to no resistance. The forces landed as planned to secure a beachhead, and a radio message was sent to the Chef de Région, ordering him to withdraw his forces to barracks, or the ships would bombard the town. The troops did indeed return to barracks, and the radio station was captured at 09:00, but not before a message was sent saying, "English landed in Tuléar". They later discovered that the French had scattered large tree stumps over the runways at the nearby airfield to render it unusable.

Only about eighty Vichy soldiers and officers were stationed at Tuléar, all of whom were captured. The town had significant defensive positions, but it was later learned that over two hundred troops had left Tuléar shortly before the landing.

Engelbrecht was under orders from Platt to placate the French after taking Tuléar. He was careful to ensure that only the South African flag was flown, not the Union Jack, and he offered to hoist the French Tricolour alongside it. He allowed the local officials to stay in post and guaranteed their salaries, and released the prisoners on parole. These measures and others allowed him to secure their cooperation, making administration of the area much simpler.

On 3rd November, the South African troops started advancing from Tuléar to Ihosy. Roadblocks — some formed by enormous boulders that had to be blasted by engineers — and weak or damaged bridges slowed progress. They made it to within a hundred kilometres of Ihosy by the time hostilities ceased.

15

ADVANCE ON FIANARANTSOA

The Allied forces in Tananarive prepared to head south, to trap Annet and his men between themselves and the forces due to land at Tuléar. Number 3 Fighting Group, now comprising three companies of King's African Rifles, three troops of armoured cars, a battery of artillery, and engineers, probed the defences at Behenjy on the night of 25th/26th September.

There were three lines of defence at Behenjy and the Allies believed that there was a battalion of troops manning them, but in fact the defenders numbered only one company. Number 3 Fighting Group called down an artillery barrage upon the first line on the morning of the 26th, and followed this with an attack by a company of infantry, who discovered that the French had abandoned the defences.

The armoured cars took the lead and came under fire from the second line of defences. After three hours of fighting, this line was taken and the Vichy forces fell back to the third line. The artillery, armoured cars, and mortars from the infantry bombarded the line, and the defenders retreated once more.

The advance continued the next day. The engineers took the lead so that they could clear obstacles. The vegetation to either side of the roads was too thick for the units to go around, so they had to remove every roadblock, which involved a lot of hard, slow, manual work. Local labour was used to help, just as the Vichy forces had enlisted the locals to help create the obstacles. This led to the odd situation that in many cases the same people who had helped the Vichy French create the roadblocks then helped the Allies remove them.

Intelligence had reported that the next resistance would be at Sambaina. As the lead unit approached, a Morane-Saulnier 406 fighter strafed them, wounding one man. They continued their advance and came under mortar fire, which killed an officer and wounded five men. The Africans responded with their own mortars before falling back as darkness fell. The next morning the Africans advanced to find the Vichy defensive position was deserted.

From Sambaina, the fighting group moved on to Antsirabe, where they arrived on the afternoon of 2nd October 1942. They remained at Antsirabe while the rest of the brigade caught up. By this time, Ihosy was the only airfield left to the Vichy forces, and South African Beauforts attacked it twice on 8th October. They discovered six Vichy aircraft there and damaged all of them with bombs and machine gun fire.

The advance resumed on 9th October with Number 2 Fighting Group taking the lead. With the neutralisation of the final Vichy fighter aircraft at Ihosy, the South African Air Force could now provide close air support to the ground troops. The railway from Tamatave was mostly working, easing supply issues. Despite calls from Annet to resist the Allies, the local population generally avoided confrontation.

At about 15:00, after advancing forty-five kilometres, the column encountered its first opposition when a concealed machine gun ambushed them, killing two and wounding eight. The next resistance was just north of Ilaka, where the column stopped for the night. There was some sniping from the hills until patrols went out to clear the area. The column entered Ilaka at 09:00 the next day. Locals warned them that a Vichy force was on the hills to the south, overlooking the road. That afternoon, the King's African Rifles attacked the Vichy positions from the front and rear, taking thirty prisoners for no losses.

Number 2 Troop of the armoured cars led the advance south towards Ambositra. The lead car entered Tsarasao-tra, but a 65mm gun hit the second car as it approached the village. The troop commander, Lieutenant Meyer, was in this vehicle, and he and his driver were both wounded. Four infantrymen riding on the car were killed, and an officer and several infantrymen were wounded. Two machine guns, concealed in the same copse of trees as the artillery piece, also began firing. Another armoured car was damaged, and a troop carrier destroyed.

Meyer's radio operator, Trooper Joubert, got Meyer and the injured infantry officer to safety, then retrieved the vehicle's first aid box. Having done that, he returned to the armoured car once more to use the radio to inform the squadron leader of the ambush. For these brave actions under enemy fire, he was awarded the Distinguished Conduct Medal.

The third armoured car in Meyer's troop fired on the

copse with its machine gun, and a force from the King's African Rifles attacked. They captured the artillery gun and its crew, and the advance continued.

On the morning of 13th October, the Africans encountered a defensive line at Ambohipia. A platoon of infantry probed it, but was pushed back. Three companies of the King's African Rifles, supported by a battery of artillery, took the position. The fighting group continued on, and encountered another defensive line shortly after, at Antanjona. A company of infantry attacked but was repulsed.

25-pounders of the King's African Rifles in action near Ambositra

An artillery barrage was brought down on the position for thirty minutes, and an infantry attack followed, supported by the armoured cars. The bombardment had evidently sapped the will of the defenders, many of whom retreated. The Africans took the position without any further difficulty, and captured over two hundred French and Malagasy soldiers.

They encountered another defensive position on 15th October at Andriamanalina, a little way south of Ambositra, where the road passed between sheer heights. The Vichy troops were dug in on the high ground overlooking the road. Local information and aerial reconnaissance revealed that the defenders had artillery, mortars, and machine guns. The strength of the defenders was uncertain, but it looked like a significant concentration of troops, and therefore a rare opportunity to deliver a powerful blow against Annet's forces.

Patrols were sent out while the rest of the fighting group came up. They discovered that machine gun posts had been sited to prevent the positions being outflanked, but they also found a way to counter this by making a wide detour. A plan was formed to have two battalions of the King's African Rifles attack from the flanks, while the main force attacked from the north, trapping the Vichy forces in a pincer. Three artillery batteries would provide support for the attack.

The 1/6th Battalion moved off at 02:00 on 17th October, making a difficult trek through the hills, man-handling all their equipment. At dawn a dense mist descended and it began to rain, reducing visibility so much that the leading company virtually walked into a machine gun post. This was taken, but two men were killed and two wounded. They reached the first objective that evening with no further trouble other than a few snipers. They resumed their march early on the morning of 18th October, and were ready for the attack by the early morning of the 19th. Meanwhile, 5th Battalion had probed the French right flank in preparation for the attack.

At 03:00 on 19th October, the armoured cars set off. Heavy mist meant that progress was very slow, with one man from each crew dismounted and giving directions to the driver. Nonetheless, they were in position at the designated time of 04:35, when the supporting artillery began their twenty-minute barrage. The armoured cars set off again at 04:50, but encountered a bridge blocked by a stone wall at 05:00. A Squadron's commander, Major Vos, examined the wall and called for men to help him remove it, but they came under machine gun fire. Major Vos repeatedly exposed himself to fire to locate the enemy position, then directed the gunners, who were able to silence the French machine gun. For this and other actions, he was subsequently awarded the Military Cross.

The mist that had made the armoured car advance so difficult worked in favour of the two flank battalions, allowing them to take the French by surprise. Meanwhile, the armoured cars supported the frontal infantry attack. The bombardment was the heaviest used in the Madagascar campaign, and this, along with the surprise flank attack and the discovery that their retreat was cut off, led to the French forces' surrender at 08:30.

The Allies had indeed delivered a powerful blow to the Vichy forces. They had captured over seven hundred men, two 75mm artillery guns, and many mortars and machine guns, with no casualties to themselves. Colonel Metras, the local French commander, surrendered. Annet now had only eight companies remaining, and no heavy artillery. But he still refused to give up, much to the delight of the Vichy government, which reported to the German Armistice Commission that Madagascar was mounting a "heroic resistance" against the Allied forces.

On 20th October, the advance was resumed with 1/6th Battalion of the King's African Rifles taking the lead. Once more they encountered many roadblocks, all of which had to be removed, taking a great deal of time and effort.

About six kilometres south of Ambohimahasoa, the road forked. The main road passed through a Vichy position at Mandalahy. The other road was less well defended, but was a longer route. Brigadier Dimoline, the commander of 22nd East African Brigade, decided to split his forces. Number 2 Fighting Group took the longer route, while the rest of the brigade advanced on Mandalahy.

Number 2 Fighting Group faced fewer roadblocks and found that the bridges they had to cross were still intact, despite being prepared for demolition. On the main road, however, all the bridges had been destroyed. Patrols captured a deserter from the Mandalahy position, and his interrogation, combined with aerial reconnaissance, gave the Allies a good picture of the defences they were facing.

The Vichy forces consisted of three infantry companies, dug in on ridges overlooking the road. Dimoline planned to deliver a feint, with air support, against the western position, which was held by one company. The 1/6th Battalion of the King's African Rifles, with artillery support, would attack the two companies holding the eastern position. This was planned for the morning of 29th October.

Number 2 Fighting Group meanwhile had completed its drive down the longer road, and turned to support the rest of the brigade in its attack on Mandalahy. They captured the French commanding officer, Colonel Tricoire, and his staff in their command post. Tricoire refused to order his troops to surrender, and so the rest of the attack went ahead.

At 03:00 the infantry moved into position, and the artillery barrage began at 04:35. Advancing under cover of the artillery, the Allies took the defenders completely by surprise. By noon the positions were under Allied control, and they had taken around one hundred prisoners. An infantry company travelled by train to the harbour town of Manakara, which was taken without any resistance.

The Brigade now turned its attention to Fianarantsoa, the old capital of Madagascar, which Annet had retreated to after the fall of Tananarive. Advance units reached the town in the afternoon of 29th October, and it surrendered without a fight. They had taken eight hundred prisoners between Mandalahy and Fianarantsoa, which meant that Annet had very few men left under his command. Malagasy troops were deserting in large numbers, but Annet still showed no sign of surrendering. He was now at Ihosy, another two-hundred-kilometre drive south from Fianarantsoa.

16

SURRENDER AND OCCUPATION

Number 2 Fighting Group set off from Fianarantsoa on 2nd November. Aerial reconnaissance had discovered a Vichy defensive position at Vatoavo and roadblocks being set up, so they expected further opposition. In the afternoon, the headquarters staff of the Vichy artillery surrendered at the Talata-Ampana monastery. They'd had nothing left to command since 19th October, when they'd lost their remaining artillery pieces at Andriamanalina.

During the 3rd, the King's African Rifles cleared the road to Vatoavo, and on the morning of the 4th, they climbed the heights in front of the village. Immediately, the Vichy defenders opened fire with mortars and machine guns. The Allies responded with artillery, and white flags soon appeared among the defensive positions. The position was a strong one, but the commander had received orders from Annet to surrender.

On 5th November, Annet's representative arrived at Dimoline's headquarters to request surrender terms. It was exactly eight weeks since the landings at Majunga.

Hostilities ceased at 14:00, but Annet's negotiator wasted time, so that he finally signed the surrender just after midnight on 6th November 1942. This meant that the Madagascar campaign had lasted six months, so the French servicemen were eligible for a campaign medal and enhanced pension. Churchill announced the signing of the armistice in parliament on 10th November.[1]

22nd East African Brigade had achieved a remarkable victory, defeating an enemy of roughly double their size. An enemy, moreover, that was defending familiar country and able to choose its positions. Despite all that, they took over 3,000 prisoners, sixteen artillery pieces, and fifty heavy machine guns. Their own losses to enemy action during the eight-week campaign were only twenty-seven killed and eighty-two wounded.

Allied losses were generally light, totalling only 142 killed or wounded. Malaria took a much greater toll on most units, although the men of the 22nd East African Brigade suffered little from the disease.

Following Annet's surrender, the issue of who should administer the island, the British or the Free French, came to a head. The British had failed to formulate a solid, coherent policy regarding administration of the island. The original intention was that British control would be limited and brief, but Churchill started to use it as a bargaining chip with de Gaulle and the French National Committee, which made the island's future far less certain. Differences between the Foreign Office, the War Office, and the Chiefs of Staff exacerbated the problem. Grafftey-Smith summed up the issue when he complained that the occupation did not have a "clear and consistent policy governing relations between the occupying power on the one hand and the local adherents of

Marshal Pétain and General de Gaulle respectively on the other."[2]

Finally, in a war cabinet meeting on 9th November 1942, Churchill noted that de Gaulle had been "most co-operative" regarding operations in North Africa, and therefore an early announcement should be made that civil administration would be handed over to the French National Committee.[3] The war cabinet agreed, although they wanted some slight changes to the communique that was to be issued. For military purposes, however, Madagascar would be under Platt's East African Command, and the fortress of Diego Suarez a separate military zone under direct British control.

General Legentilhomme, who had previously served on Madagascar, formally took over civil administration of the island on 8th January 1943. He strived, with some success, to increase production of strategic raw materials, notably mica and graphite, which was the island's primary contribution to the Allied war effort. Legentilhomme stayed in the post until May 1943, when Pierre de Saint-Mart took over.

Saint-Mart was an experienced civil colonial administrator, and this was reflected in increased production of raw materials for the Allies. Unfortunately, the French National Committee were reluctant to promise greater independence for Madagascar after the war. This soured his relations with the local population, significantly limiting what he was able to achieve.

17

CONCLUSION

The invasion of Madagascar was controversial in 1942, and with hindsight it seems that the fear of the Japanese basing naval forces at Diego Suarez was unfounded. However, Operation Ironclad gave the Allies a victory at a point in the war when there was little else for them to cheer about. That may seem like a frivolous thing to spend lives and money on, but every general knows that troop morale is important, and a good politician knows that civilian morale is important when conducting a war.

Once the British had taken Diego Suarez, they had to take the rest of the island, despite their initial refusal to accept this reality. Not doing so would have required shipping of supplies onto the island, making it the burden that Churchill was so keen to avoid.

Operation Ironclad was the first major amphibious operation conducted by the Allies, and they learned some useful lessons from the experience. This notable success has been overshadowed by Operation Jubilee, the disastrous raid at Dieppe, which came a few months later. The lessons of Ironclad were not applied to Jubilee, at least partly due to the lack of time between the two operations. The lessons of Ironclad did help later amphibious operations, however. Difficulties faced landing vehicles and men onto beaches led the Allies to form Combined Operations Pilotage Parties (COPPs) to undertake reconnaissance of enemy beaches prior to an assault. The Tank Landing Ship (LST) concept was proved at Madagascar, and the type was of major importance in later operations in Europe and the Far East. In addition, Ironclad was an early example of assault sweeping, the practice of clearing naval mines ahead of an invading force, and the British repeated the use of dummy paratroopers during the invasion of France in 1944.

The planners of later amphibious operations, including the much more famous invasion of Normandy in 1944, owed a great deal to the men that fought in Madagascar. Ironclad showed that it was not necessary to attack a major port directly. Rather, it was possible to land large forces on beaches away from the coastal defence batteries that were commonly situated around ports. Once landed, those forces could then march on the port and attack from the landward side.

Madagascar was the only time that Tetrarch tanks saw combat in the light tank role that they were originally designed for. They are much better known for their role in Operation Overlord, where they served as airborne tanks, transported in large Hamilcar gliders.

Operation Ironclad showed that SOE could provide valuable intelligence and support for an invasion. The organisation always had enemies in the British government, and their early successes in Madagascar helped fend them off, at least for a time. Their part in Operation

Line was much less successful however, which gave fuel to their enemies. Percy Mayer's capture in Diego Suarez had dealt a severe blow to SOE's effectiveness on the island.

With Mayer's cover blown, SOE sent a new senior agent named Richard Broad to take over Mayer's role in the occupied sector. Mayer and Broad did not get on well, and Broad did not have Mayer's extensive local knowledge. On top of this, General Platt did not like SOE[1]. The War Office had a tendency to issue instructions to SOE without Platt's knowledge, which made matters worse. All of these factors meant that the tasks assigned to SOE in preparation for Streamline Jane may have been overly ambitious, but SOE probably felt that they couldn't refuse, and with no paratroopers available to take the bridges, there was little alternative.

The Earl of Selborne, the Minister for Economic Warfare, recommended Percy Mayer for an OBE, and his wife Berthe for an MBE. A mistaken belief by some officials that Berthe was French (she wasn't, but Percy had dual British/French citizenship) caused some delay, and in April 1943 Field Marshal Smuts pursued it, saying that they both deserved "very great personal recognition" which was already "far too long delayed." SOE received the insignia later that month, but the Earl of Selborne insisted that the OBE should be presented to Mayer by King George himself. In June, the King presented Mayer with the OBE and an MBE for his wife. Since Mayer was still an active SOE agent, the ceremony had to be held in private. Lord Harlech, the High Commissioner to South Africa, presented the MBE to Berthe Mayer on 22nd November 1943, in what an SOE report described as "quite an impressive little ceremony"[2].

It wasn't all positive, of course. The British consistently

underestimated the strength of Vichy opposition. They never seemed to fully understand that although France had started the war as an ally, Vichy France was not, and in fact could be entirely hostile to British and Allied interests. Indeed, the Vichy government was able to use the resistance in Madagascar as proof to the Germans that they were willing to fight against their former ally. Conversely, the Madagascar campaign highlighted the coolness of relations between Britain and the Free French.

Operations Stream and Jane meant that landing craft were not available for Wavell's offensive against the Japanese in Burma. He had to abandon plans for an amphibious operation to capture airfields on Akyab Island when the landing craft were diverted to Madagascar. When de Gaulle first mooted the idea of invading Madagascar, he had suggested taking Majunga and Tananarive, not Diego Suarez. Had that plan been adopted, the campaign might have been shorter, reducing the impact on the Far East. That's speculation, of course, but it is certainly true that the plan to take Diego Suarez was based on a mistaken belief that there was no need to occupy the entire island.

The capture of this apparently insignificant island influenced the wider war in ways that are not immediately obvious. Raw materials necessary for munitions production, and which were in short supply for the Allies, were present on the island. In particular, graphite was needed for various war industries, most notably the atomic weapons programme at Los Alamos. Almost immediately after the capture of the capital, arrangements were being made to ship several thousand tons of graphite to the UK and the US.

This was indeed a strange campaign, as Sir John

Hammerton described it in the contemporaneous book *The Second Great War*. The combatants had started the war as allies. The British clung onto their hope that there would be no need for fighting. The French (both Vichy and Free French) never fully let go of the old imperial antagonism, and were always suspicious that an opportunistic Britain intended to expand her empire at France's expense. The locals often worked equally hard for both sides, helping the French set up roadblocks, then helping the Allies remove them. It's not clear why. Maybe they thought the war wasn't relevant to them, or perhaps they thought one colonial power was much the same as another.

I shall give the last word on the campaign to Winston Churchill. In *The Hinge of Fate*, the fourth volume of his Second World War history, he wrote:

> "The Madagascar episode was in its secrecy of planning and precision of tactical execution a model for amphibious descents. The news arrived at a time when we sorely needed success. It was in fact for long months the only sign of good and efficient war direction of which the British public were conscious."[3]

APPENDIX I: FORCES INVOLVED IN OPERATION IRONCLAD

Force F

Battleship
  Ramillies

Aircraft Carriers

  Indomitable

- 800 Squadron (Eight Fairey Fulmars)
- 806 Squadron (Four Fairey Albacores)
- 827 & 831 Squadrons (Twenty-four Albacores)
- 880 Squadron (Nine Hawker Sea Hurricanes)

  Illustrious

- 810 & 829 Squadrons (Twenty Fairey Swordfish)
- 881 Squadron (Twelve Grumman Martlets)
- 882 Squadron (Eight Martlets and one Fulmar)

Cruisers

Devonshire
Hermione

Destroyers

Javelin
Laforey
Lightning
Lookout
Pakenham
Paladin
Panther

Corvettes

Auricula
Cyclamen
Freesia
Fritillary
Genista
Jasmine
Nigella
Thyme

Minesweepers

Cromarty
Cromer
Poole
Romney

Assault Transports

Karanja
Keren
Royal Ulsterman
Winchester Castle
Sobieski (Polish)

Specialised Ships

Bachaquero (LST)
Derwentdale (LCA)

Troopships

Duchess of Atholl
Franconia
Oronsay

Stores and Motor Transport ships

Thalatta
City of Hong Kong
Empire Kingsley
Mahout
Martand
Nairnbank
Greystoke Castle (arrived at Diego Suarez on 7 May with stores and ammunition)

Fleet Auxiliary

Easedale (tanker)

Hospital Ship

Atlantis

Force 121

Headquarters

Royal Engineers detachment
Signals Section
Royal Army Service Corps
Royal Army Medical Corps
Royal Army Ordnance Corps
Pay Corps detachment
Provost detachment
Pioneer detachment

29th Independent Infantry Brigade

Headquarters 29th Independent Infantry Brigade
Defence Platoon
Signals Section
1st Battalion Royal Scots Fusiliers
2nd Battalion Royal Welch Fusiliers
2nd Battalion East Lancashire Regiment
2nd Battalion South Lancashire Regiment
Half squadron, B Special Service Squadron, Royal Armoured Corps
Half squadron, C Special Service Squadron, Royal Armoured Corps
455 Independent Light Battery, Royal Artillery
145 Light Anti-Aircraft Troop, Royal Artillery

236 Field Company, Royal Engineers (less one section)

17th Infantry Brigade

Headquarters 17th Infantry Brigade
Defence Platoon
Signals Section
Light Aid Detachment
2nd Battalion Royal Scots Fusiliers
2nd Battalion Northamptonshire Regiment
6th Battalion Seaforth Highlanders
9th Field Regiment, Royal Artillery
38th Field Company, Royal Engineers
141 Field Ambulance, Royal Army Medical Corps

13th Infantry Brigade

2nd Battalion The Cameronians
2nd Battalion Royal Inniskilling Fusiliers
2nd Battalion Wiltshire Regiment
91st Field Regiment, Royal Artillery
252 Field Company, Royal Engineers
13th Infantry Brigade Company, Royal Army Service Corps
164 Field Ambulance, Royal Army Medical Corps

Number 5 (Army) Commando

South African Air Force Units

32 Coastal Reconnaissance Flight (Five Martin Marylands)

36 Coastal Reconnaissance Flight (Six Bristol Beauforts)

37 Coastal Reconnaissance Flight (Five Beauforts and one Maryland)

50 Transport Flight (Six Junkers Ju 52s)

53 Transport Flight (Six Lockheed Lodestars)

54 Transport Flight (Six Lodestars)

French Forces

2me Regiment Mixte de Madagascar (Mixed Madagascar Regiment)

1er Bataillon

2me Bataillon

3me Bataillon

Detachment de Reconnaissance Motorise

Groupe Campaigne et Montagne (Field and Mountain Artillery Group)

Coastal Artillery

Anti-Aircraft Artillery

French Deployments

Windsor Castle/Courrier Bay:

One combat group with one 60mm mortar

One 138mm coastal battery

One infantry section

Ampasindava:

One infantry section

Cap Diego Peninsula:

One infantry company
One 65mm anti-tank section
One 240mm coastal battery
Two 75mm naval guns

Joffre Line:

One infantry battalion
Four 75mm anti-tank guns

Camp d'Ambre:

Four-man outpost with radio

Camp du Sakaramy:

Two infantry companies

Arrachart Airfield:

One 75mm battery

Orangea Peninsula:

One infantry company

Camp d'Ankorika:

One infantry company

Fort d'Ankorika:

Two 80mm field guns

Mamelon Vert:

Two 80mm field guns

Le Point de Vue:

One 164mm coastal battery

Poste Optique/Sémaphore d'Orangéa:

One 100mm coastal battery

Cap Miné:

One 320mm coastal battery

Plage d'Orangéa:

Three 47mm naval guns

Diego Suarez:

One infantry company
One 75mm field battery
One 75mm mobile field section

One 65mm mobile anti-tank section
One 75mm coastal gun (at lighthouse)
Two 90mm anti-aircraft guns
One 13.2mm anti-aircraft section

French Naval Forces

Diego Suarez anchorage:

Bougainville (auxiliary cruiser)
Bévéziers (submarine)
D'Entrecasteaux (colonial sloop)

Majunga:

Glorieux (submarine)

At sea:

D'Iberville (colonial sloop)
Le Héros (submarine)
Le Monge (submarine)

Aircraft (Arrachart Airfield)

Three Potez 63
Five Morane-Saulnier 406
Two Potez 25

APPENDIX II: ULTIMATUM TO THE GOVERNOR OF DIEGO SUAREZ

On Board the British Flagship,
3rd May, 1942.

Your Excellency,

The strategic position of Diego Suarez requires that it should not fall into the hands of the Japanese and that the territory should be available for those forces which are fighting to restore freedom in the world and secure the liberation of France and French territory. It cannot be allowed to suffer the fate of Indo China.

I therefore request that in order that bloodshed may be avoided you will surrender the territory under your control to me unconditionally and instruct your officials and Armed Forces to obey the orders which I shall issue.

The action which I am now taking on the instruction of H.M. Government has the full approval of the Government of the United States.

In order to assist you in reaching a favourable decision I have been instructed by H.M. Government to inform you of the following:—

1. Diego Suarez is French and will remain French, and will be restored to France after the war. H.M. Government have repeatedly made it clear that they do not covet an inch of French territory. I repeat this assurance.

2. Funds will be made available to meet the salaries and pensions of all personnel, Civil and Military, who elect to co-operate with the United Nations.

3. If any Civil and Military employees do not wish to co-operate, they will, provided they can claim the right to residence in Metropolitan France, be repatriated as and when shipping becomes available.

4. The trade of Diego Suarez with the United Nations will be restored. H.M. Government will extend to Diego Suarez all the economic benefits accorded to French territories which have already joined the United Nations.

5. There must be no destruction of Civil and Military installations, W/T Stations, War Stores, etc. Those responsible for any such sabotage will not benefit by conditions (2) and (3) above.

Your reply to this communication should be sent to me immediately in plain language by radio on 500 kc/s (600 metres) using call sign GBXZ.

Alternatively it should be sent by hand of officer under flag of truce to the Officer Commanding Occupying Troops.

I am, Your Excellency

E. N. SYFRET.
Rear-Admiral and Commander-in-Chief, British Forces.
His Excellency,
The Governor of Diego Suarez.

APPENDIX III: FORCES INVOLVED IN OPERATION STREAMLINE JANE

Force M

Battleship
   Warspite

Cruisers

   Birmingham
   Caradoc
   Dauntless
   Gambia

Anti-Aircraft ship

   Heemskerck

Aircraft carrier

   Illustrious

- Six Fairey Fulmars
- Eighteen Fairey Swordfish
- Twenty-one Grumman Martlets

Monitor

Erebus

Headquarters ship

Albatross

Fast Minelayer

Manxman

Destroyers

Napier
Tjerk Hiddes
Van Galen
Active
Arrow
Blackmore
Fortune
Foxhound
Hotspur
Inconstant
Nepal
Nizam
Norman

Minesweepers

Cromarty
Cromer
Freesia
Romney

Anti-submarine Whalers

Lurcher
Mastiff
Sigfar

Netlayer

Brittany

Assault Ships

Dilwara
Dunera
Empire Pride

Motor Transport Ships

Advisor Charlton Hall
Delius
Empire Squire
Gascony
Ocean Vesper
Ocean Viking
Ross
Wanderer

Personnel Ships

> *Abosso*
> *Empire Trooper*
> *Empire Woodlark*
> *Khedive-Ismail*
> *Llandaff Castle*

Oilers

> *British Energy*
> *Doryssa*
> *Easedale*
> *Eaglesdale*

Petrol tanker

> *Kola*

Hospital ships

> *Dorsetshire*
> *Vasna*

Allied Land Forces

29th Independent Infantry Brigade

> Headquarters 29th Independent Infantry Brigade
> Defence Platoon
> Signals Section
> 1st Battalion Royal Scots Fusiliers

2nd Battalion Royal Welch Fusiliers

2nd Battalion East Lancashire Regiment

2nd Battalion South Lancashire Regiment

Half squadron, B Special Service Squadron, Royal Armoured Corps

Half squadron, C Special Service Squadron, Royal Armoured Corps

455 Independent Light Battery, Royal Artillery

145 Light Anti-Aircraft Troop, Royal Artillery

236 Field Company, Royal Engineers (less one section)

Number 5 (Army) Commando

A Squadron, 1st Armoured Car Commando, South African Tank Corps

22nd (East Africa) Infantry Brigade

1/1 Battalion (Nyasaland), King's African Rifles

5th Battalion (Kenya), King's African Rifles

1/6 Battalion (Tanganyika), King's African Rifles

56th (Uganda) Field Battery, East African Artillery

9th Field Regiment, Royal Artillery

60th Field Company, East African Engineers

5th (Kenya) Field Ambulance

Allied Shore-Based Aircraft

Six Martin Marylands

Eight Bristol Beauforts

Five Westland Lysanders

Six Fairey Albacores

Six Fairey Fulmars

Eight Supermarine Walrus
Seven Consolidated Catalinas

French Forces

Note: there were two Régiment Mixte de Malgache (1er and 2em), but sources list all the battalions as being from the 1er Regiment. I have been unable to determine which battalions were from the 2em Regiment.

West Coast

Two platoons of reservists and volunteers at Nossi-bé
Two companies of the 1er Régiment Mixte de Malgache (Mixed Madagascar Regiment) at Ambanja
One battalion of the 1er Régiment Mixte de Malgache at Majunga

East Coast

One battalion of the 1er Régiment Mixte de Malgache at Tamatave
One artillery section (65mm) at Tamatave
One company of the 1er Régiment Mixte de Malgache at Brickaville

Centre of the Island

Three battalions of the 1er Régiment Mixte de Malgache at Tananarive
One motorised reconnaissance detachment at Tananarive

Emyrne battery at Tananarive

One artillery section (65mm) at Tananarive

One engineer company at Tananarive

One company of the 1er Régiment Mixte de Malgache at Mevatanana

One company of the Bataillon de Tirailleurs Malagaches at Fianarantsoa

South of the Island

One company of the Bataillon de Tirailleurs Malagaches at Fort dauphin

One company of the Bataillon de Tirailleurs Malagaches at Tuléar

Aircraft (Ivato Airfield)

Six Potez 63

Eleven Morane-Saulnier 406

APPENDIX IV: PRINCIPAL PERSONALITIES

British

General Alan Brooke: Chief of the Imperial General Staff, chairman of the Chiefs of Staff Committee, and military advisor to Winston Churchill

Winston Churchill: Prime Minister and Minister of Defence

Brigadier Dimoline: Commander of 22nd East African Brigade

Anthony Eden: Foreign Secretary

Brigadier Frank Festing: Commander of 29th Independent Infantry Brigade

Lord Harlech: High Commissioner to South Africa

Berthe Mayer: SOE agent on Madagascar and Percy Mayer's wife

Percy Mayer: SOE agent on Madagascar and Berthe Mayer's husband

Roundell Palmer, Earl of Selborne: Minister for Economic Warfare

Lieutenant-General Sir William Platt: General Officer Commanding East Africa Command

Major J.E.S. Simon: Tank squadron commander

Field Marshal Jan Smuts: Prime Minister of the Union of South Africa

Major-General Robert Sturges: Royal Marines General. Commander of land forces for Operation Ironclad

Admiral Edward Neville Syfret: Overall commander of Operation Ironclad

French

Governor Armand Annet: Governor-General of Madagascar from April 1941

Colonel Claerebout: Commander of Diego Suarez

Jules Marcel de Coppet: Governor of Madagascar

Admiral Darlan: Chief of Staff of the French Navy, then Minister of Marine in the Vichy French government

Brigadier-General Charles de Gaulle: Leader of Free France, the French government-in-exile set up in Britain after the surrender of France

General Guillemet: Senior military commander on Madagascar

General Legentilhomme: Free French Governor-General of Madagascar, 1942–1943

Captain Maerten: Naval Commandant at Diego Suarez and commander of the French navy in Madagascar

Marshal Pétain: Leader of the Vichy French government, established after France surrendered to Germany

Paul Reynaud: Prime Minister, March–June 1940

Pierre de Saint-Mart: Free French Governor-General of Madagascar from 1943

General Weygand: Commander of the French army in 1940, then Vichy Minister for Defence

Other Nationalities

Fricke, Admiral, German naval chief of staff

Nomura, Vice Admiral, Japanese naval attaché in Berlin

APPENDIX V: PLACE NAMES

Throughout this book, I have used contemporary place names, as used in 1942. Several places referenced in the book are now known by new names. These places are listed below with their modern name.

Akyab Island (Burma): Sittwe Island (Myanmar)

Burma: Myanmar

Ceylon: Sri Lanka

Diego Suarez: Antsiranana

French Indochina: Vietnam

Hell-Ville: Andoany

Joffreville: Ambohitra

Majunga: Mahajanga

Nossi-bé: Nosy Be

Tamatave: Toamasina

Tananarive: Antananarivo

Tuléar: Toliara

Sakaramy: Ambia

ABOUT RUSSELL PHILLIPS

Russell Phillips writes books and articles about military technology and history. Born and brought up in a mining village in South Yorkshire, they have lived and worked in South Yorkshire, Lincolnshire, Cumbria and Staffordshire. Russell has always had a deep interest in history and conflicts all over the world, and enjoys sharing their knowledge with others through clear, factual accounts which shine a light on events of the past.

Their articles have been published in *Miniature Wargames*, *Wargames Illustrated*, *The Wargames Website*, and the Society of Twentieth Century Wargamers' *Journal*. They have been interviewed on *BBC Radio Stoke*, *The WW2 Podcast*, *Cold War Conversations*, and *The Voice of Russia*. They currently live in Stoke-on-Trent with their wife and two children.

 twitter.com/RPBook

 facebook.com/RussellPhillipsBooks

 goodreads.com/RussellPhillips

ALSO BY RUSSELL PHILLIPS

A Ray of Light: Reinhard Heydrich, Lidice, and the North Staffordshire Miners

The Bear's Claws: A Novel of World War III

Operation Nimrod: The Iranian Embassy Siege

The Bear Marches West: 12 Scenarios for 1980s NATO vs Warsaw Pact Wargames

A Fleet in Being: Austro-Hungarian Warships of WWI

A Damn Close-Run Thing: A Brief History Of The Falklands War

This We'll Defend: The Weapons and Equipment of the U.S. Army

Weapons and Equipment of the Warsaw Pact

Tanks and Combat Vehicles of the Warsaw Pact

Combat Engineering Equipment of the Warsaw Pact

Artillery of the Warsaw Pact

Weapons and Equipment of the Warsaw Pact: Volume One

DIGITAL REINFORCEMENTS: FREE EBOOK

To get a free ebook of this title, simply go to shilka.uk/dr and enter code SCMA27.

The free ebook can be downloaded in several formats: Mobi (for Kindle devices & apps), ePub (for other ereaders & ereader apps), and PDF (for reading on a computer). Ereader apps are available for all computers, tablets and smartphones.

NOTES

1. Introduction

1. MoI No. 42, Daily Report on Morale, 5 July 1940
2. MoI No. 43, Daily Report on Morale, 6 July 1940

2. Concerns about Madagascar

1. 'Madagascar: Bribing of French Naval Commander', 1942 1941. HS 3/28. The National Archives, Kew.
2. Harrison, E. D. R. 'British Subversion in French East Africa, 1941-42: SOE's Todd Mission'. The English Historical Review 114, no. 456 (1999): 339–69.
3. '1. Atlantic Islands and Madagascar. Part of COS(41)427th Meeting.', 18 December 1941. CAB 79/55/84. The National Archives, Kew.
4. Churchill, Winston. The Hinge of Fate. The Second World War 4, 1950.

3. Planning

1. Harrison, E. D. R. 'British Subversion in French East Africa, 1941-42: SOE's Todd Mission'. The English Historical Review 114, no. 456 (1999): 339–69.
2. Churchill, Winston. The Hinge of Fate. The Second World War 4, 1950.

4. Operation Ironclad

1. Roskill, Captain Stephen. The Period of Balance. History of the Second World War: The War at Sea 2, 1956.

6. Attack on Diego Suarez, 5th May

1. Wallace, Samuel. 'Arme Blanche to Armoured Warfare: The Process of Mechanisation within the British Cavalry and the Construction of British Tank Doctrine, c.1925-45', 2017.
2. 'Letter from Major Simon, B Special Service Squadron', 16 May 1942.
3. 'Recommendation for Award for Grimes Rank: Serjeant Service No: 7696560 ...', 1943 1941. WO 373/29/103. The National Archives, Kew.

7. Diego Suarez, 6th May

1. 'Capture of Diego Suarez'. London Gazette, 4 March 1948.
2. Benbow, Tim. 'History Extra Podcast, September 2012'. Mp3.

8. Joffre Line Forts and the Orangea Peninsula

1. 'Reports on Operation IRONCLAD', 1942. HS 3/23. The National Archives, Kew.
2. Roskill, Captain Stephen. The Period of Balance. History of the Second World War: The War at Sea 2, 1956.
3. Roskill, Captain Stephen. The Period of Balance. History of the Second World War: The War at Sea 2, 1956.
4. Harrison, E. D. R. 'British Subversion in French East Africa, 1941-42: SOE's Todd Mission'. The English Historical Review 114, no. 456 (1999): 339–69.
5. 'Notes From Theatres of War No.8 and No.9'. The War Office, October 1942.
6. 'Operation IRONCLAD (Invasion of Madagascar): SOE Support HS 3/22', 1942. HS 3/22. The National Archives, Kew.
7. Chiefs of Staff. Telegram to Special...', 3 May 1942. FO 954/18A/36. The National Archives, Kew.
8. Steenkamp, Willem. The Black Beret: The History of South Africa's Armoured Forces - Beginnings to the Invasion of Madagascar 1942. Vol. 1. 2 vols. 1. Helion, 2016.

9. "Live and Let Live"

1. Churchill, Winston. The Hinge of Fate. The Second World War 4, 1950.
2. 'Operations: Operation IRONCLAD (Madagascar): Chiefs of Staff. Telegram to Special...', 3 May 1942. FO 954/18A/36. The National Archives, Kew.
3. Churchill, Winston. The Hinge of Fate. The Second World War 4, 1950.
4. Jennings, Eric T. 'Vichy Propaganda, Metropolitan Public Opinion, and the British Attack on Madagascar, 1942'. L'Esprit Créateur 47, no. 1 (2007): 44–55.
5. Jennings, Eric T. 'Vichy Propaganda, Metropolitan Public Opinion, and the British Attack on Madagascar, 1942'. L'Esprit Créateur 47, no. 1 (2007): 44–55.
6. Grehan, John. Churchill's Secret Invasion: Britain's First Large Scale Combined Operations Offensive 1942, 2013.
7. 'Abyssinia, East Africa and Madagascar', 1943 1941. HS 3/9. The National Archives, Kew.
8. Churchill, Winston. The Hinge of Fate. The Second World War 4, 1950.
9. 'Operations: Operation IRONCLAD (Madagascar): Prime Minister Minute to Secretary of State...', 2 June 1942. FO 954/18A/61. The National Archives, Kew.
10. 'Operations: Operation IRONCLAD (Madagascar): From Lord Harlech (South Africa)...', 6 June 1942. FO 954/18A/71. The National Archives, Kew.
11. '5 Commando', December 1942. WO 218/36. The National Archives, Kew.

10. Operation Streamline Jane

1. 'Operations: Operation IRONCLAD (Madagascar): General Smuts to Prime Minister Conference...', 21 June 1942. FO 954/18A/76. The National Archives, Kew.
2. Kirby, Major-General S. Woodburn. The War Against Japan. History of the Second World War: War against Japan 2, 1958.
3. 'Madagascar - Future Policy.', 28 July 1942. CAB 79/56/77. The National Archives, Kew.
4. 'Record Type: Memorandum Former Reference: WP (42) 350 Title: Madagascar -...', 10 August 1942. CAB 66/27/30. The National Archives, Kew.

11. Operation Stream

1. 'Burma 1942: Royal Armoured Corps: B Squadron Special Service', December 1942. WO 172/707. The National Archives, Kew.
2. Wall, Colonel Dudley. Operation Ironclad: The Madagascar Campaign 1942, 2006.

12. Operation Line

1. Harrison, E. D. R. 'British Subversion in French East Africa, 1941-42: SOE's Todd Mission'. The English Historical Review 114, no. 456 (1999): 339–69.
2. 'Second Combined Operation against Madagascar (Operations STREAM, LINE and JANE) HS 3/27', 1942. HS 3/27. The National Archives, Kew.
3. 'Operation "Streamline Jane": War Book', September 1942. WO 106/3612. The National Archives, Kew.
4. MoI Digital and TNA. 'MoI Weekly Report, 29 September 1942', 29 September 1942.
5. Smith, Colin. England's Last War Against France: Fighting Vichy 1940-42. Accessed 21 August 2019.

13. Operation Jane

1. 'Burma 1942: Royal Armoured Corps: B Squadron Special Service', December 1942. WO 172/707. The National Archives, Kew.

16. Surrender and Occupation

1. 'MADAGASCAR (OPERATIONS) (Hansard, 10 November 1942)'. Accessed 28 August 2020. https://api.parliament.uk/historic-hansard/commons/1942/nov/10/madagascar-operations.
2. Thomas, Martin. 'Imperial Backwater or Strategic Outpost? The British Takeover of Vichy Madagascar, 1942'. The Historical Journal 39, no. 4 (1996): 1049–74.
3. 'Cabinet Conclusions', 9 November 1942. CAB 65/28/21. The National Archives, Kew.

17. Conclusion

1. Harrison, E. D. R. 'British Subversion in French East Africa, 1941-42: SOE's Todd Mission'. The English Historical Review 114, no. 456 (1999): 339–69.
2. 'Madagascar: Honours and Awards', 1943 1942. HS 3/29. The National Archives, Kew.
3. Churchill, Winston. The Hinge of Fate. The Second World War 4, 1950.

BIBLIOGRAPHY

'1. Atlantic Islands and Madagascar. Part of COS(41)427th Meeting.', 18 December 1941. CAB 79/55/84. The National Archives, Kew.

'1. Construction of an Aerodrome in the Faroes. 2. Establishment of a Radio Telephone...', 28 September 1942. CAB 79/23/24. The National Archives, Kew. https://discovery.nationalarchives.gov.uk/details/r/C9191294.

'1. MADAGASCAR - EQUIPMENT FOR UNION BRIGADE. 2. MADAGASCAR - WITHDRAWAL OF SOUTH...', 4 June 1942. CAB 79/21/19. The National Archives, Kew.

'1. Operation "TORCH" - Discussion with Colonel Eddy. 2. Operation "TORCH" - General...', 11 August 1942. CAB 79/56/86. The National Archives, Kew.

'1 Royal Scots Fusiliers', December 1942. WO 174/33. The National Archives, Kew.

'2 Cameronians (Scottish Rifles)', June 1942. WO 174/28. The National Archives, Kew.

'2 Royal Inniskilling Fusiliers', May 1942. WO 174/29. The National Archives, Kew.

'2 Royal Scots Fusiliers', June 1942. WO 174/34. The National Archives, Kew.

'2 South Lancashire Regiment (Prince of Wales's Volunteers)', December 1942. WO 174/31. The National Archives, Kew.

'2 Wiltshire Regiment (Duke of Edinburgh's)', May 1942. WO 174/37. The National Archives, Kew.

'5 Commando', December 1942. WO 218/36. The National Archives, Kew.

'9 Field Regiment, Royal Artillery', November 1942. WO 174/19. The National Archives, Kew.

'19 Field Battery, Royal Artillery', October 1942. WO 174/21. The National Archives, Kew.

'38 Field Company, Royal Engineers', June 1942. WO 174/38. The National Archives, Kew.

'91 Field Regiment, Royal Artillery', May 1942. WO 174/20. The National Archives, Kew.

'Abyssinia, East Africa and Madagascar', 1943 1941. HS 3/9. The National Archives, Kew.

Benbow, Tim. 'D-Day Dress Rehearsal: The Battle for Madagascar'. BBC History Magazine, September 2012. https://www.historyextra.com/period/second-world-war/d-day-dress-rehearsal-the-battle-for-madagascar/.

———. 'History Extra Podcast, September 2012'. Mp3, n.d. https://www.historyextra.com/period/second-world-war/d-day-dress-rehearsal-the-battle-for-madagascar/.

The Ninth Queen's Royal Lancers, 1936-1945: The Story of an Armoured Regiment in Battle

Bright, Joan, ed. The Ninth Queen's Royal Lancers, 1936-1945: The Story of an Armoured Regiment in Battle. S.l.: Naval & Military Press, 2020. https://www.naval-military-press.com/product/ninth-queens-royal-lancers-1936-45the-story-of-an-armoured-regiment-in-battle/.

'Burma 1942: Royal Armoured Corps: B Squadron Special
Service', December 1942. WO 172/707. The National
Archives, Kew.

'Cabinet Conclusions', 9 November 1942. CAB 65/28/21.
The National Archives, Kew. https://discovery.nation-
alarchives.gov.uk/details/r/C9156299.

'Capture of Diego Suarez'. London Gazette, 4 March 1948.
https://www.thegazette.co.uk/London/issue/38225/supplement.

Churchill, Winston. The Hinge of Fate. The Second World
War 4, 1950.

'Defence Plan for Diego Suarez. COS(42)89(O).', 8 April
1942. CAB 79/56/22. The National Archives, Kew.
https://discovery.nationalarchives.gov.uk/details/r/C9192118.

'Extract From 9th Queens Royal Lancers 1936-1945', n.d.

'FRANCE: To Mr Peake (Despatch No 183). Talk with de
Gaulle about Madagascar.', 11 May 1942. FO 954/8A/229.
The National Archives, Kew.

Furrutter, Karl. 'WarWheels.Net -A Brief History of the
Marmon Herrington Range of Armoured Cars by Karl
Furrutter'. WarWheels.net. Accessed 17 December 2019.
http://www.warwheels.net/MarmonHerringtonAChistory-
FURRUTTER.html.

Grainger, John D. Traditional Enemies: Britain's War With
Vichy France 1940-42, n.d.

Grehan, John. Churchill's Secret Invasion: Britain's First
Large Scale Combined Operations Offensive 1942, 2013.
https://books2read.com/u/3LpN8X.

Hammerton, Sir John. The Second Great War, Volume 6.
Vol. 6. The Second Great War, n.d.

Harrison, E. D. R. 'British Subversion in French East
Africa, 1941-42: SOE's Todd Mission'. The English Historical Review 114, no. 456 (1999): 339–69.

Horrabin, J. F. Horrabin's Atlas-History of the Second

Great War, January 1942 to July 1942. 1st ed. Vol. 6. 9 vols. London: Thomas Nelson & Sons Ltd, 1942.

———. Horrabin's Atlas-History of the Second Great War, July 1942 to January 1943. 1st ed. Vol. 7. 9 vols. London: Thomas Nelson & Sons Ltd, 1943.

Jennings, Eric T. 'Vichy Propaganda, Metropolitan Public Opinion, and the British Attack on Madagascar, 1942'. L'Esprit Créateur 47, no. 1 (2007): 44–55.

'Joubert DCM'. London Gazette, 22 December 1942, sec. Supplement:35830.

'KAR MM Awards: Sergeant Odilo, Sergeant Walasi, Corporal Rabson'. London Gazette, 24 November 1942, sec. Supplement:35799.

Kirby, Major-General S. Woodburn. The War Against Japan. History of the Second World War: War against Japan 2, 1958.

Ladd, J.D. Assault from the Sea, 1939-45. Endeavour Press, 2015.

'Letter from Major Simon, B Special Service Squadron', 16 May 1942.

'Lieutenant-Commander John Michael Hodges RN and Captain Price RM Award of DSO', 25 August 1942. https://www.thegazette.co.uk/London/issue/35679/page/3715.

Lloyd, Cliff. Operation Ironclad: The British Invasion of Madagascar - 1942, n.d.

'Madagascar - Future Policy.', 28 July 1942. CAB 79/56/77. The National Archives, Kew.

'Madagascar: Bribing of French Naval Commander', 1942 1941. HS 3/28. The National Archives, Kew.

'Madagascar: Honours and Awards', 1943 1942. HS 3/29. The National Archives, Kew.

'MADAGASCAR (OPERATIONS) (Hansard, 10 November 1942)'. Accessed 28 August 2020. https://api.parliament.uk/historic-hansard/commons/1942/nov/10/madagascar-operations.

'Madagascar Orders of Battle'. Accessed 29 December 2020. http://france1940.free.fr/vichy/ob_mada.html.

Manley, David. 'Operation Menace - Anglo-French Combined Ops 1940'. SOTCW Journal, Autumn 2001.

'Middle East: Foreign Office Telegram to Accra, No 21. Operation STREAM.', 5 September 1942. FO 954/15A/211. The National Archives, Kew.

MoI Digital. 'MoI No. 42, Daily Report on Morale, 5 July 1940', 5 July 1940. http://www.moidigital.ac.uk/reports/home-intelligence-reports/morale-summaries-of-daily-reports-part-b-inf-1264/idm140465681452832/.

'MoI No. 43, Daily Report on Morale, 6 July 1940', 6 July 1940. http://www.moidigital.ac.uk/reports/home-intelligence-reports/morale-summaries-of-daily-reports-part-b-inf-1264/idm140465681166400/.

MoI Digital and TNA. 'MoI Weekly Report, 6 May 1942', 6 May 1942. http://www.moidigital.ac.uk/reports/home-intelligence-reports/home-intelligence-weekly-reports-inf-1-292-1-2/idm140465679357216/.

MoI Digital and TNA. 'MoI Weekly Report, 6 October 1942', 6 October 1942. http://www.moidigital.ac.uk/reports/home-intelligence-reports/home-intelligence-weekly-reports-inf-1-292-1-2/idm140465671486384/.

MoI Digital and TNA. 'MoI Weekly Report, 11 May 1942', 11 May 1942. http://www.moidigital.ac.uk/reports/home-intelligence-reports/home-intelligence-weekly-reports-inf-1-292-1-2/idm140465681770192/.

MoI Digital and TNA. 'MoI Weekly Report, 15 September 1942', 15 September 1942. http://www.moidigital.ac.uk/reports/home-intelligence-reports/home-intelligence-weekly-reports-inf-1-292-1-2/idm140465670658048/.

MoI Digital and TNA. 'MoI Weekly Report, 18 May 1942', 18 May 1942. http://www.moidigital.ac.uk/reports/home-intelligence-reports/home-intelligence-weekly-reports-inf-1-292-1-2/idm140465681323136/.

MoI Digital and TNA. 'MoI Weekly Report, 22 September 1942', 22 September 1942. http://www.moidigital.ac.uk/reports/home-intelligence-reports/home-intelligence-weekly-reports-inf-1-292-1-2/idm140465670990064/.

MoI Digital and TNA. 'MoI Weekly Report, 29 September 1942', 29 September 1942. http://www.moidigital.ac.uk/reports/home-intelligence-reports/home-intelligence-weekly-reports-inf-1-292-1-2/idm140465671181040/.

Moulton, Major-General J.L. 'Madagascar: First of the Allied Invasions'. Purnell's History of the Second World War, n.d.

'Notes From Theatres of War No.8 and No.9'. The War Office, October 1942.

'Operation IRONCLAD (Invasion of Madagascar): SOE Support HS 3/21', 1942. HS 3/21. The National Archives, Kew.

'Operation IRONCLAD (Invasion of Madagascar): SOE Support HS 3/22', 1942. HS 3/22. The National Archives, Kew.

'Operation Ironclad; Madagascar'. Accessed 21 August 2019. https://www.combinedops.com/MADAGASCAR.htm.

The Soldier's Burden. 'Operation Line'. Accessed 1 July 2020. http://www.kaiserscross.com/188001/611143.html.

'Operation "Streamline Jane": War Book', September 1942. WO 106/3612. The National Archives, Kew.

'Operations: Operation IRONCLAD (Madagascar): Chiefs of Staff. Telegram to Special...', 3 May 1942. FO 954/18A/36.

The National Archives, Kew. https://discovery.nation-alarchives.gov.uk/details/r/C6562662.

'Operations: Operation IRONCLAD (Madagascar): From Lord Harlech (South Africa)...', 6 June 1942. FO 954/18A/71. The National Archives, Kew.

'Operations: Operation IRONCLAD (Madagascar): From War Cabinet Offices (Brigadier...', 29 April 1942. FO 954/18A/30. The National Archives, Kew.

'Operations: Operation IRONCLAD (Madagascar): General Smuts to Prime Minister Conference...', 21 June 1942. FO 954/18A/76. The National Archives, Kew.

'Operations: Operation IRONCLAD (Madagascar): Prime Minister Minute to Secretary of State...', 2 June 1942. FO 954/18A/61. The National Archives, Kew. https://discovery.-nationalarchives.gov.uk/details/r/C6562676.

'Operations: Operation IRONCLAD (Madagascar): Prime Minister to Admiral Syfret....', 14 May 1942. FO 954/18A/40. The National Archives, Kew.

Chazfest. 'Percy Mayer'. Accessed 4 September 2020. https://chazfest.com/portfolio-items/percy-mayer/.

'Percy Mayer Award of MC'. London Gazette, 28 August 1945, sec. Supplement:37244.

'Percy Mayer MC Recommendation', 1945. WO 373/98/430. The National Archives, Kew.

perspectivesonafrica. 'Operation Ironclad: The British Invasion of Madagascar in 1942'. Perspectivesonafrica (blog), 24 December 2011. https://perspectivesonafrica.-wordpress.com/2011/12/24/operation-ironclad-the-british-invasion-of-madagascar-in-1942/.

'Recommendation for Award for Martin, J Rank: Serjeant Service No: 3384378 ...', 1943 1941. WO 373/29/136. The National Archives, Kew.

'Recommendation for Award for Odilo Rank: Serjeant

Service No: 11636 ...', 1943 1941. WO 373/29/137. The National Archives, Kew.

'Recommendation for Award for Rabson Rank: Corporal Service No: 12669 ...', 1943 1941. WO 373/29/139. The National Archives, Kew.

'Recommendation for Award for Vos, Frederick Wilhelm Gabriel Rank: Temporary...', 1943 1941. WO 373/29/156. The National Archives, Kew.

'Recommendation for Award for Walasi Rank: Serjeant Service No: 11947 ...', 1943 1941. WO 373/29/138. The National Archives, Kew.

'Recommendation for Award for Grimes Rank: Serjeant Service No: 7696560 ...', 1943 1941. WO 373/29/103. The National Archives, Kew.

'Record Type: Memorandum Former Reference: WP (42) 350 Title: Madagascar -...', 10 August 1942. CAB 66/27/30. The National Archives, Kew.

'Relations with Vichy (Prints)', November 1940. PREM 3/186A/3. The National Archives, Kew.

'Reports on Operation IRONCLAD', 1942. HS 3/23. The National Archives, Kew.

Rigge, Simon. War in the Outposts. Time-Life Books, 1980. https://www.worldcat.org/title/war-in-the-outposts/oclc/1087622473.

Roskill, Captain Stephen. The Period of Balance. History of the Second World War: The War at Sea 2, 1956.

'Second Combined Operation against Madagascar (Operations STREAM, LINE and JANE) HS 3/26', 1942. HS 3/26. The National Archives, Kew.

'Second Combined Operation against Madagascar (Operations STREAM, LINE and JANE) HS 3/27', 1942. HS 3/27. The National Archives, Kew.

Smith, Colin. England's Last War Against France: Fighting

Vichy 1940-42. Accessed 21 August 2019. https://book-s2read.com/u/b5QqJG.

Fourie, Major D. F. S., ed. 'Operation Rose: The Only Amphibious Landing by South African Forces at War MADAGASCAR 1942'. South African Military History Society Journal 2, no. 1 (June 1971). http://samilitaryhistory.org/vol02ice.html.

Steenkamp, Willem. The Black Beret: The History of South Africa's Armoured Forces - Beginnings to the Invasion of Madagascar 1942. Vol. 1. 2 vols. 1. Helion, 2016. https://www.helion.co.uk/military-history-books/the-black-beret-the-history-of-south-africas-armoured-forces-volume-1-beginnings-to-the-invasion-of-madagascar-1942.php.

'THE SOUTH AFRICAN AIR FORCE IN THE MADAGASCAR CAMPAIGN, 1942 - South African Military History Society Journal'. Accessed 1 March 2021. http://samilitaryhistory.org/vol092jc.html.

Wallace, Angus. 'The WW2 Podcast: 125 - Mechanisation of British Cavalry Units and Tank Doctrine'. Mp3. Accessed 15 September 2020. https://ww2podcast.com/ww2-podcast/125-mechanisation-of-british-cavalry-units-and-tank-doctrine/.

Thomas, Martin. 'Imperial Backwater or Strategic Outpost? The British Takeover of Vichy Madagascar, 1942'. The Historical Journal 39, no. 4 (1996): 1049–74.

Treadwell, Terry C. Strike from beneath the Sea: A History of Aircraft-Carrying Submarines. 1st ed. Stroud: Tempus Publishing, 1999.

'Vichy France', 1942 1940. DO 35/1001/6. The National Archives, Kew.

Wall, Colonel Dudley. Operation Ironclad: The Madagascar Campaign 1942, 2006. https://issuu.com/dudley1/docs/abf_madagascar_ww_ii.

Wallace, Samuel. 'Arme Blanche to Armoured Warfare:
The Process of Mechanisation within the British Cavalry
and the Construction of British Tank Doctrine, c.1925-45',
2017. https://doi.org/10.13140/RG.2.2.26538.36805.

Wessels, Andre. 'South Africa and the War against Japan
1941-1945'. South African Military History Society Journal
10, no. 3 (June 1996).

http://samilitaryhistory.org/vol103aw.html.

INDEX